time *for* dinner

time *for* dinner

STRATEGIES, INSPIRATION, AND RECIPES FOR FAMILY MEALS EVERY NIGHT OF THE WEEK

BY  EDITORS

PILAR GUZMÁN, JENNY ROSENSTRACH, AND ALANNA STANG

PHOTOGRAPHY BY
MARCUS NILSSON

RECIPES BY
VICTORIA GRANOF

DESIGN BY
NUMBER 17, NYC

PRODUCED BY
 MELCHER MEDIA

PUBLISHED BY
CHRONICLE BOOKS
SAN FRANCISCO

LIBRARY OF CONGRESS CATALOGING-IN-PUBLICATION DATA AVAILABLE.

THE INFORMATION IN THIS BOOK HAS BEEN CAREFULLY
RESEARCHED AND TESTED, AND ALL EFFORTS HAVE BEEN MADE
TO ENSURE ACCURACY. NEITHER THE PUBLISHER
NOR THE CREATORS CAN ASSUME RESPONSIBILITY FOR
ANY ACCIDENT, INJURIES, LOSSES, OR
OTHER DAMAGES RESULTING FROM THE USE OF THIS BOOK.

ISBN: 978-0-8118-7742-8

MANUFACTURED IN CHINA

10 9 8 7 6 5 4 3 2 1

CHRONICLE BOOKS LLC
680 SECOND STREET, SAN FRANCISCO, CALIFORNIA 94107
WWW.CHRONICLEBOOKS.COM

DEDICATED TO
the beyond-talented staff
of *Cookie* magazine.

What you are holding in your hands is more parenthood playbook than cookbook. It takes into account that some days, you feel like Supermom, ready to prep for four days' worth of meals; and some days, it's all you can do to slather a little peanut butter and jelly on bread and, yes, call it dinner. **WHAT ARE YOU IN THE MOOD TO MAKE TONIGHT? USE THESE CHAPTER TITLES TO HELP FIGURE IT OUT.**

The idea of this cookbook evolved very naturally. As friends for more than a decade and fellow editors who launched *Cookie*, the lifestyle magazine for parents, we've watched each other's children go from breast-feeding to bike riding. In person, on the phone, and over e-mail, many of our exchanges have fallen under the category of what we've come to call "food therapy": a mutual recitation of the previous night's dinner with the kids. *Did he try the black beans? Is spinach back on the green-light list? Were you able to braise the pork chop without pushing bedtime too late?*

But the more we discussed our dinners, the more we realized how many of our own—and our friends' and readers'—conversations were consumed by the stress and logistics, and (less often, perhaps) by the joy of feeding our respective broods. Why? Because whether we're in the make-it-from-scratch or the frozen-food camp, the pleasure of feeding our kids a delicious meal is often replaced by the business of getting the protein-veg-carb triumvirate dutifully down the hatch. Now that we're parents, those of us who once relished shopping for a single meal from four specialty markets register a wistful disconnect with our former, food-centric selves—and with this shift, we watch our yummy-mummy fantasy of serving our families a Moroccan stew turn into the reality of a not-so-yummy lunch lady serving up a waterlogged hot dog.

    This kitchen playbook takes into account that SOME DAYS YOU FEEL LIKE SUPERMOM, SOME DAYS YOU ARE EXHAUSTED, SOME DAYS YOU FULLY INTEND TO MAKE THE CHICKEN POTPIES . . . AND NEVER GET AROUND TO PICKING UP THE CHICKEN. We recognize that all these versions of you are, well, you. We understand that soccer practice will run late, and that even when you think you have your program all together, you might have to rush a headlong three-year-old who dinged his chin on the coffee table to the ER just as you have embarked on the browning stage of an ambitious coq au vin. Oh, well—there is always tomorrow.

PILAR GUZMÁN

1

THE FAMILY KITCHEN

STOCK YOUR PANTRY AND GIRD YOURSELF FOR BATTLE

You can buy up any number of cookbooks that will tell you what to cook for dinner tonight. But as parents, you know by now that the "what" part of the dinner equation is only relevant if you've figured out the "how" part first. As in, *HOW* DO I LOGISTICALLY AND PHYSICALLY GET THE MEAL ON THE TABLE WHEN I HAVE A TODDLER HANGING ON MY APRON BEGGING TO BE READ A STORY, or pleading to "help" with the stirring? And once the meal is produced, *how* do I get that toddler and her older and younger siblings to actually consume it? Think of this chapter as a parent's "how headquarters." In it, you'll find all the gear and goodies you'll need to keep the kids occupied while you cook, ideas to engage them (constructively) in the process, and finally strategies to convince even the most manipulative little monster to take a bite.

THE ESSENTIAL PANTRY
You'll see these ingredients over and
over again in our recipes. Turn the page
to learn about their secret powers.

BAKING MIXES 1

KOSHER SALT 2

PEANUT BUTTER 3

HONEY 4

CUMIN 5

RED-PEPPER FLAKES 6

CHINESE FIVE-SPICE 7
POWDER

CINNAMON 8

CURRY 9

BAY LEAVES 10

ROSEMARY 11

PANCAKE MIX 12

SOY SAUCE 13

VINEGARS 14

FLOUR & GRAINS 15

16 PASTAS

17 BEANS

18 CANNED TOMATO PRODUCTS

19 PANKO CRUMBS

20 COCONUT MILK

21 RAISINS

22 OLIVE OIL

23 TUNA

24 NUTS

25 FLAXSEEDS

26 COUSCOUS

27 RICE

28 WONDRA FLOUR

29 CORNFLAKE CRUMBS

30 QUINOA

31 CHICKEN BROTH

1

BAKING MIXES
You only make other moms feel bad when you bake the classroom cupcakes from scratch anyway.

17

BEANS
It's not just their nutritional content that makes them a superfood—they're cheap, easy, and endlessly flexible.

HONEY
Pooh's favorite doubles as a cough syrup (with a squeeze of lemon) and soothes cuts and burns.

4

7

CHINESE FIVE-SPICE POWDER
Both sweet and zesty, it's the magic fairy dust of spices.

12

PANCAKE MIX
For weekend breakfasts and for vegetable fritters! (*See page 235.*)

29

CORNFLAKE CRUMBS
For replicating the chicken fingers they will inexplicably only eat at the restaurant—until now. (*See page 112.*)

14

CIDER VINEGAR
Takes away the itch when applied directly on a mosquito bite!

18

CANNED TOMATO PRODUCTS
Embrace his pizza-and-pasta-only diet—stock up on good-quality sauces, purees, and whole peeled tomatoes.

16

PASTAS
Tuesday she likes macaroni; Wednesday she'll only eat wagon wheels. There is no such thing as having too many pasta options.

20

COCONUT MILK
Mix it into rice, barley, chicken soup, whatever. It literally sweetens the deal every time.

25

FLAXSEEDS
Sprinkle them onto his bowl of granola for an extra shot of omega-3s; toss a handful of ground flax into breading for chicken cutlets.

NUTS
They may be banned at school, but they're loaded with protein, healthy fats, and fiber, so hand them out freely at home if you can.

24

28

WONDRA FLOUR
Dredge white fish in it (mixed with salt and pepper) then pan-fry it at high heat to give it the golden deliciousness they expect.

TIP
Clip package labels and shove them in the jars to help you identify the grains and flours inside.

30

QUINOA
Cooked in a big batch on Sunday and stored in the fridge, it's the perfect fall-back side dish.

THE ESSENTIAL FRIDGE
It's all about easy access for the kids.

POMEGRANATE JUICE 1

KETCHUP 2

PINE NUTS 3

STRING CHEESE 4

YOGURT TUBES 5

GINGER ALE 6

BAKING SODA 7

MAYO 8

ORANGE JUICE 9

WHIPPED CREAM 10

CHERRIES 11

GRENADINE 12

BEER 13

MAPLE SYRUP 14

SCALLIONS 15

MUSHROOMS 16

17 BLUEBERRIES

18 CHICKEN BROTH

19 BACON

20 CHEDDAR

21 PARMESAN

22 SWISS

23 TOFU

24 EGGS

25 MILK

26 GROUND TURKEY

27 GRAPE TOMATOES

28 CARROTS

29 HOT DOGS

30 PEPPERS

31 CELERY

32 FRESH HERBS

33 GREEN BEANS

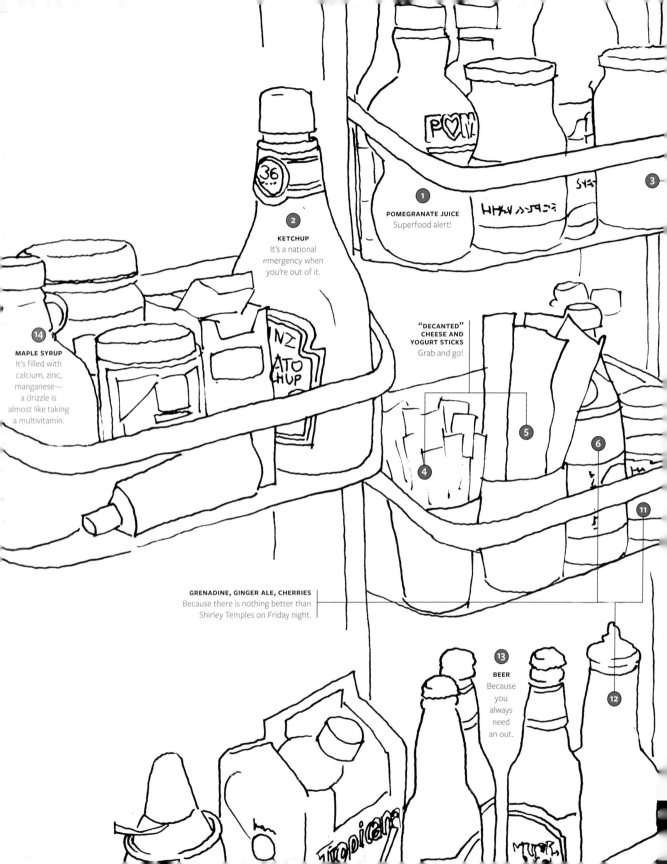

1
POMEGRANATE JUICE
Superfood alert!

2
KETCHUP
It's a national emergency when you're out of it.

14
MAPLE SYRUP
It's filled with calcium, zinc, manganese—a drizzle is almost like taking a multivitamin.

"DECANTED" CHEESE AND YOGURT STICKS
Grab and go!

GRENADINE, GINGER ALE, CHERRIES
Because there is nothing better than Shirley Temples on Friday night.

13
BEER
Because you always need an out.

PINE NUTS
Toasted or tossed in, they add buttery goodness without the butter to soups, salads, pastas, stews, etc. P.S. Don't forget to tell the kids they come from pinecones!

GROUND TURKEY
Whenever possible, get dark ground turkey. It's so much more flavorful than white turkey meat and still dramatically lower in fat than ground beef.

EGGS
The fridge is always full if you have them.

BLUEBERRIES
Vitamins C and E and fiber. Antioxidants galore. Especially alluring for toddlers who have mastered their "pincher grasp."

FRUIT
Cut up pineapple, melon, or watermelon, or place whole fruit on a low shelf to make it as grabbable as a bag of Goldfish crackers.

Milk

THE ESSENTIAL FREEZER

Whether filled with expressed breast milk or last Sunday's microwaveable Bolognese, the freezer is your peace of mind.

PEAS 1

EDAMAME 2

PIZZA DOUGH 3

BREAST MILK 4

SWEET-POTATO FRIES 5

PUREE & FLAVOR CUBES 6

SOUPS & SAUCES 7

WHOLE-WHEAT BUNS 8

LEAF SPINACH 9

COOKIE-DOUGH ROLLS 10

BACON 11

CORN 12

BERRIES 13

COFFEE 14

MEAT & POULTRY 15

2

EDAMAME
The ready-in-three-minutes snack they inhale like popcorn.

5

SWEET-POTATO FRIES
The side that's both starch and veggie—i.e., one less thing to think about.

13

BERRIES
Summery smoothies in the dead of winter— or anytime they crave a "milk shake."

9

LEAF SPINACH
Frozen chopped spinach is leaf, stems, and all. If you want only leaf, get only leaf.

4

BREAST MILK
"Money in the bank."

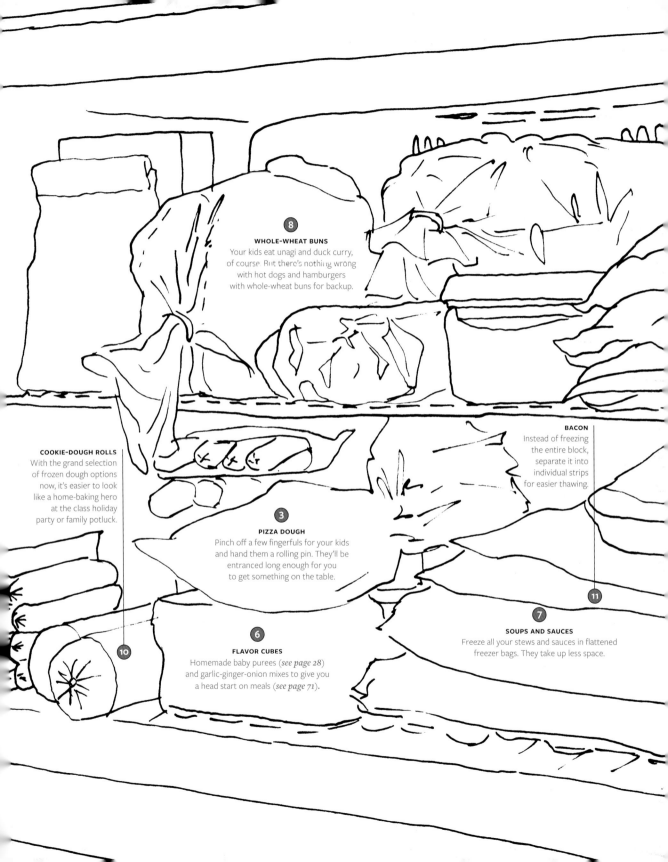

8

WHOLE-WHEAT BUNS
Your kids eat unagi and duck curry, of course. But there's nothing wrong with hot dogs and hamburgers with whole-wheat buns for backup.

BACON
Instead of freezing the entire block, separate it into individual strips for easier thawing.

COOKIE-DOUGH ROLLS
With the grand selection of frozen dough options now, it's easier to look like a home-baking hero at the class holiday party or family potluck.

3

PIZZA DOUGH
Pinch off a few fingerfuls for your kids and hand them a rolling pin. They'll be entranced long enough for you to get something on the table.

11

7

SOUPS AND SAUCES
Freeze all your stews and sauces in flattened freezer bags. They take up less space.

10

6

FLAVOR CUBES
Homemade baby purees (*see page 28*) and garlic-ginger-onion mixes to give you a head start on meals (*see page 71*).

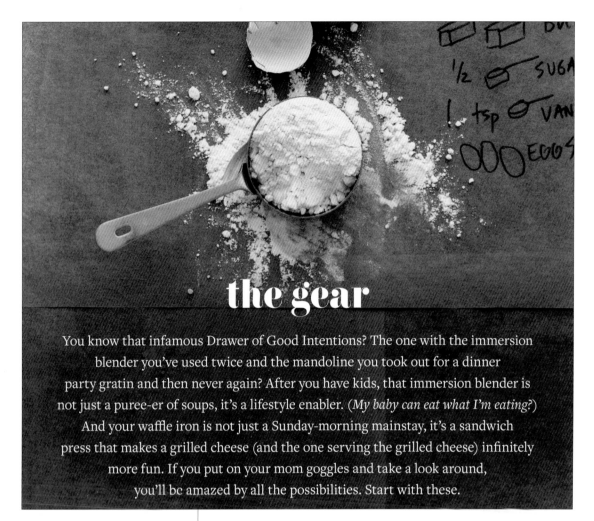

the gear

You know that infamous Drawer of Good Intentions? The one with the immersion blender you've used twice and the mandoline you took out for a dinner party gratin and then never again? After you have kids, that immersion blender is not just a puree-er of soups, it's a lifestyle enabler. (*My baby can eat what I'm eating?*) And your waffle iron is not just a Sunday-morning mainstay, it's a sandwich press that makes a grilled cheese (and the one serving the grilled cheese) infinitely more fun. If you put on your mom goggles and take a look around, you'll be amazed by all the possibilities. Start with these.

DRY MEASURING CUPS When the kids are old enough to bake with you, use these (especially the ones connected on a ring) instead of a single one. They'll have an easier time matching the fractions on the cups with fractions in the recipe. To help them along, you can also write the recipe on a piece of parchment paper with pictures and instructions.

MANDOLINE Sometimes it's not the ingredients that are instigating the tableside rejections, it's the preparation. Instead of baking a sweet potato, turn it into sweet-potato chips (any setting on the mandoline will do). Ditto for apples, potatoes, carrots, and zucchini.

STEP STOOL Not exactly a cooking tool, but probably the most important piece of gear in the effort to get kids to contribute. How else would they reach the mixing bowl? Or learn to fill their own glasses of water? Speaking of which, you can eke out endless moments of distraction when you pull a stool close to the sink and give them unbreakable bowls to "wash" under the faucet.

WAFFLE IRON Indispensable for weekend waffles, of course, but also delightful for days when a regular old pan-flipped grilled cheese just won't cut it.

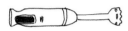

IMMERSION BLENDER Keep it on the countertop during the solid-food introductory months. It will get them started down the path of eating what you're eating. Just pick a few pieces from your plate and give them a whirl, adding pureed vegetables, formula, or breast milk to help liquefy. (See the following page for exact instructions.)

SELTZER MAKERS The kids are keeping us honest these days, thanks to the greening of their curricula, which among other things teach them about how plastic bottles are overwhelming our landfills. This contraption for homemade soda and "bubble water" means less waste—and more high-fives from the young eco-cops.

SIBLING EQUALIZERS Pancake-batter dispensers make perfectly round pancakes come out pretty much the same size every time, handily eliminating any disputes over who gets the bigger one. Ditto the hand mixer with two beaters. For two-kid families, licking the beater has never been more just.

SALAD SPINNER It's so rare to find the task that is genuinely enjoyable for them and genuinely helpful for you. The pull-cord type is fun, but you can't go wrong with the pump version either. (It's also a good idea to pick up old spinners at garage sales—they come in handy for makeshift spin-art projects.)

SERVING PLATTERS When you're outsourcing the serving control to the kids, it's crucial to have a wide selection of platters. Square, oval, melamine, china—it makes no difference, as long as you can display an array of beautiful foods for the taking.

the solid-food rollout*

To optimize your chances of raising a child who eats the same things
you do (i.e., all the recipes in this cookbook), you'll want to start
them on real food as early as possible. You'll know it's time for something
more than milk when baby starts grabbing at the goodies on your plate.
Yes, you can always pop open a jar, but preparing your own healthy and delicious
baby food is not as hard as you may think—especially when Mom and Dad
get something out of it, too. On the following pages, you'll find 10 simple,
nutrient-packed purees that also happen to lend themselves to
grown-up dishes (and even cocktails!) you'll want to get all grabby over, too.

*Plus, what's in it for you.

GETTING STARTED

timing

Start slowly: Don't introduce more than one new food every four days. As exciting as it is to see your baby's reaction to a first taste, it's better to be sure he has no problem with it—either allergic or digestive—before adding another item to the menu. And limit new-food feedings to once a day, early in the day. It's not a good idea to give the baby something he hasn't ever tried in the late afternoon or evening, because if he does have complications, you'll be dealing with them in the middle of the night.

quantity

A little goes a long way. Even though your baby may seem hungry all the time, remember that his stomach is about the size of his fist—and that he still has to learn how to swallow. Give him time to get used to the texture and taste of something other than milk in his mouth by starting with just one or two teaspoons for several days, until he is clearly eager for more. Then gradually increase the quantity over the course of a few weeks.

consistency

The first solid foods should be anything but solid, as baby is still learning to relax his tongue-thrust reflex. You can liquefy any puree by adding water, breast milk, or formula. Once he has the hang of swallowing, you can serve slightly thicker purees by using less water, reducing a water puree over heat, or blending a puree with rice or oatmeal cereal.

preparation

With a few notable exceptions, like **bananas** and **avocados,** the fruits and vegetables on the next few pages require cooking before being pureed. You can use a steamer basket or just plop the chopped ingredient in a pan with some water, then steam or simmer until tender. **Potatoes** and **squash** can be oven-roasted and then scooped from their skins before being pureed. Stone fruit (**peaches, plums, apricots**) should be scored with a tiny "x" on the bottom end, plunged into boiling water for a minute to loosen the skin, dipped in a bowl of icy water, and then peeled before being pureed. A food processor or blender (both standing and immersion work well) makes the job of mashing much easier—especially if you're doing big batches.

WHAT'S IN IT FOR THEM:

apple

In addition to keeping the doctor away, eating plenty of apples helps babies build reserves of vitamins A and C; the mineral boron, which is important for bone health; and quercetin, a powerful antioxidant.

avocado

The avocado's baby-friendly buttery flesh is an excellent source of oleic acid, one of the "good fats" that promote healthy brain and muscle building and help prevent cancer. It also contains tons of fiber, potassium, and red blood cell–producing folate.

butternut squash

With its bright flesh, this winter squash is tempting, tasty, and teeming with good-for-yous such as beta carotene—which is as good for the skin and the immune system as it is for the eyes—and manganese, a mineral that activates enzymes and vitamins in the body.

sweet potato *or* **yam**

Sweet potatoes are packed with dietary fiber and natural sugars in the form of complex carbs, protein, and vitamins A and C, as well as a good dose of iron and calcium. Not bad for something that tastes like candy to a baby.

peach

A perfectly ripe peach is about as close to nirvana as most of us are going to get. That's why we've never heard of a baby refusing it as a puree. Good thing, too, since the fruit's high concentration of vitamins A and C keeps baby's complexion looking, well, peachy.

cinnamon apple muffins

In case fresh applesauce is not motivation enough, you can fold apple puree into pancake batter (*see page 51*), add it to any packaged muffin mix, or serve it hot, spiked with a little calvados, over pork chops.

blender soup

Once you've smashed up enough for the kid, chuck the rest into a blender for cold buttermilk-avocado soup (*see page 85*).

butternut squash soup

Use roasted cubes for butternut squash soup (*see page 201*). Butternut squash puree is also easy to sneak into mac-and-cheese or spaghetti sauce. Just mix in a tablespoon or two before serving.

roasted sweet potato *with* miso-scallion butter

A sweet side: While the potatoes are in the oven, combine 1½ sticks of well-softened unsalted butter, 1½ tablespoons of miso paste (preferably white), and 3 tablespoons of chopped scallion. Slice the hot potatoes lengthwise, pour the miso-scallion butter in the center of each, and serve.

peach bellinis

Mix 3 to 4 tablespoons of peach puree with ½ cup of chilled prosecco; enjoy a brief moment of nonparental bliss.

STAGE 2 FOODS *(for babies over 6 months old)*

pear

Since they are low in acid and high in water content, pears are ideal for babies with reflux or other digestive problems—especially constipation. If you're starting with a very soft pear, there is no need to steam it; just peel and puree.

zucchini

Zucchini—which can either be chopped and steamed or shredded and sautéed in olive oil before being pureed—is full of nutrients that help keep the digestive tract healthy. But all baby will know is that its mild flavor is easy to love, especially when mixed with other favorites like carrots, apples, or avocados.

peas

They're called sweet for a reason—the same reason babies the world over love them. They're also packed with protein (a cup has as much as a tablespoon of peanut butter) and calcium.

spinach

We all know it makes you strong to the finish. We also know that having to clean the dirt from a fresh bunch can keep you from getting started. If it seems like too much hassle to deal with fresh, go with a bag of prewashed or a thawed box of frozen organic whole leaves.

mango

Like most other tropical fruits (including bananas, papayas, kiwis, and melons), vitamin C-packed mangoes don't require any cooking. Just start with a very ripe one, peel, cut the flesh away from the pit, and puree it in a food processor.

breakfast *and/or* **dessert**

Like apple puree, mashed pear is delicious mixed into pancakes or muffins and as a side dish or sauce for braised or seared meats. It also makes an easy dessert served over ice cream or yogurt with a little chocolate drizzle.

zucchini pizza

This pizza is particularly easy to prepare if you're using the shred-and-sauté method to prepare baby's zucchini; just mix it with sautéed onions and some grated Parmesan, and your topping is ready to bake (*see page 154*).

minted-pea puree *with* **mozzarella**

Add some mint, lemon, and olive oil to baby's mashed peas, and you've got a whole new way to think about a sandwich spread (*see page 189*).

mini vegetable custards

Mini custards (*see page 221*) work just as well with pureed spinach as they do with leaves. And once you've got a batch of pureed spinach in the fridge, it's easy to slip it into eggs, tomato sauce, and curries.

mango martinis

Shake up a mango martini with 2 ounces of your puree, 2 ounces of mango juice, 2 ounces of triple sec, and 4 ounces of vodka. Or set some sliced mango aside for a grilled shrimp salad (*see page 255*).

babysitter in a box

"I want to help." These are words to make any star-chart keeper proud, but when they come from the mouth of a 3-year-old as the clock is ticking down to dinnertime, they can send you spiraling into panic. The solution? A "babysitter in a box," which contains everything kids need to feel like they're contributing and, more important, to entertain themselves for at least a good portion of your prep time. Grab a mix of the items listed here and store them in a durable bin on a low shelf, where your children can easily get to it. Next, praise them for their help—and get on with the business of dinner.

CATCHALL The bin should be large enough to feel like a treasure-filled toy chest but small enough to stash in a cupboard. Plastic is both easy to clean and indestructible.

OILCLOTH Pick up a poster-size piece at any fabric store. It's a perfect drop cloth that can be wiped down and rolled up easily.

MIXING BOWLS You'll need a big one to be the all-important cauldron, plus a bunch of small, deep ones.

POURERS Include containers that have self-regulating spouts (squeeze bottles, oil dispensers, funnels). The rookie mistake is including a measuring cup—any liquid in there will be spilled across the floor in one flick of a toddler's wrist.

CANISTERS Think variety: sifters, small-hole spice jars, and plastic canisters to hold dry goods. The name of the game is minimal parental involvement, so easy-open containers are key.

DRY GOODS Everything should be interestingly textured and capable of sitting on a shelf for a month without spoiling: rice, sugar in the raw, old Easter-egg tablets, aromatic spices (like oregano and cinnamon, a pinch of either of which will be instantly, tangibly gratifying), cake decorations, sprinkles, beans, lentils, and baking soda—which, when mixed with vinegar, will make a tremendously satisfying fizz. Note: Whatever you do, avoid flour. Its powdery texture makes it all but impossible to keep contained.

RANDOM DELIGHTS Include spoons, rolling pins (look for the tiny ones), timers, measuring spoons, colanders. FYI: Placing muffin papers into a muffin tin will probably take a toddler the same amount of time it will take you to chop an onion.

THE EXTRAS If you want to up the fun factor (read: mess factor), hand them some raw pizza dough, honey in a squeeze bottle, or food coloring. (But remember to remove them before stashing the kit.)

picky-eater emergency kit

We are not going to bore you with the rules
of how many and which kinds of chef's
knives and skillets no kitchen should be without.
What's *waaaay* more important to know when
feeding young kids (especially picky young kids) is
what to stock in your arsenal of kitchen supplies
that will help make the selling,
spinning, and surviving of dinner possible.

PARCHMENT PAPER Cooking fish in parchment paper happens to be a brilliantly simple and easily customizable way to cook an entire dinner (*see page 156*). But we also find we have great success when we use it to get the kids excited about vegetables. Place on it whatever you have (green beans, snow peas, sliced carrots, and sliced zucchini all work well); add salt, pepper, and a squeeze of lemon; and wrap it as the deli wraps a sandwich—folding the overhang underneath the contents. Bake for 8 to 10 minutes and you have "vegetable presents" that can be unwrapped with great fanfare at the table.

EGGCUP The more fun the design, the more fun the experience will be for your child, of course, but even a plain eggcup will give a humble egg the elevation you have been looking for. Try serving hard- or soft-boiled eggs in them.

SALTCELLARS AND SHOT GLASSES We don't pretend to know why, but kids have trouble resisting the minuscule. So why give them nuts in one big bowl when you can do it in two or three or four or six little ones? Ditto for drinks! Sipping their milk from two tiny glasses will feel much more surmountable than it would from one standard-size cup.

TOOTHPICKS, SKEWERS, CORN HOLDERS Try this arsenal of smallish spears with whole fruit, cubed cheddar, chopped veggies, and whole apples and watch your SRC (success rate of consumption) rise accordingly. Note: The only thing corn holders shouldn't be used with is corn. Way too predictable.

FLASHLIGHT For particularly desperate nights, kill the lights, arm your little superhero with a flashlight in one hand and a fork in the other, and have him attack any villainous last scraps of dinner to save the day.

TAKE-OUT CONTAINERS AND CHOPSTICKS Serve your "Mom! Chicken and broccoli again?" in these. Added fun: Ring the doorbell before you serve, and pretend it's a delivery. Chopsticks, of course, can be used at any time of the day on almost anything to improve your chances of success.

COCKTAIL UMBRELLAS In the milk glass or on the broccoli—there's nothing they won't upgrade. A fleet of them stuck into corn bread makes your starch look like a delightful, edible summer beach.

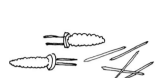

VOTIVES Set their melamine plates on one of your finer (washable) tablecloths, dim the overheads, light some candles, and call it Restaurant Night. The atmosphere might get them feeling adventurous, and the lighting might hide the parsley (a.k.a. "green stuff") you forgot to omit from the sauce.

STRAWS Swirly ones, straight ones, boring ones, colorful ones. It doesn't matter—as long as they are inserted into liquid, they will make anything more drinkable. IKEA has a rainbow pack of 200 that's so cheap it's practically free and looks particularly fun when stored in a glass jar on the countertop.

mix + match meals

On nights when the baby (or each kid) is eating a separate meal, you don't have
to serve up the fresh fish with the farmers'-market greens to guarantee everyone's
getting a nutritionally balanced dinner. Use this selection of quick-prep—or no-prep—
healthy staples from the pantry. As long as each of the categories is represented,
you can throw together any combination and feel good about it.

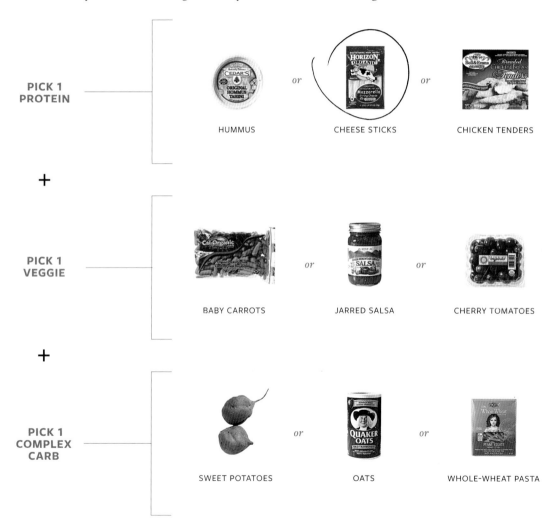

PICK 1 PROTEIN

HUMMUS   *or*   CHEESE STICKS   *or*   CHICKEN TENDERS

+

PICK 1 VEGGIE

BABY CARROTS   *or*   JARRED SALSA   *or*   CHERRY TOMATOES

+

PICK 1 COMPLEX CARB

SWEET POTATOES   *or*   OATS   *or*   WHOLE-WHEAT PASTA

Cheese stick + edamame + corn = 100% balanced dinner!

CANNED BEANS	CANNED TUNA	EGGS	TOFU HOT DOGS	NUT BUTTER
BROCCOLI	EDAMAME	OLIVES	FROZEN SPINACH	AVOCADOS
FROZEN BROWN RICE	MULTIGRAIN BREAD	BAKED BLUE-CORN CHIPS	RICE NOODLES	FROZEN CORN

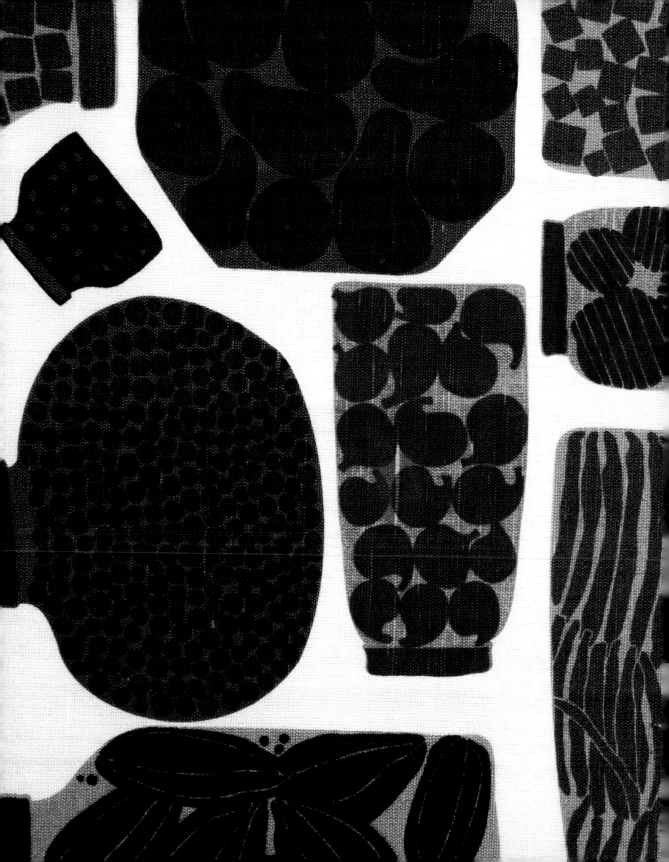

IF I COULD JUST MAKE IT TO WEDNESDAY...

A "WEEKLY" MEAL PLAN THAT ACTUALLY WORKS

Imagine a weekly meal plan that takes into account the fact that your day, well, sucked, and that the idea of turning on the stove to brown and braise that chicken you had such high hopes for when you bought it two days ago has lost all its appeal. In our minds, the only meal plan to have is the one that takes moods, kids, and real life into account. For starters, don't pretend for a second that you're going to cook from scratch every night, all week long. (Don't you know by now that just sets you up for failure?) Instead, set your sights on cooking through Wednesday. To ensure that you get even that far, prepare four easy dishes at the same time on Sunday that, served together, give you a delicious Sunday dinner and, served separately, give you building blocks for any number of scrumptious meal possibilities—including breakfasts and lunches. In this chapter, you'll find lots of ideas for meals like that, plus eight recipes that, when made on Sunday, help get you ahead of the game for the week. What about Thursday, Friday, and Saturday? Pull from the freezer, order in, scrounge up leftovers. And open a bottle of vino — YOU'VE DONE ENOUGH, AND YOU DESERVE A NIGHT (OR TWO OR THREE) OFF.

STRATEGIC SUNDAY DINNER

BRAISED PORK, ROASTED KABOCHA SQUASH, COOKED APPLES & BARLEY

BRAISED PORK

one 5-to-6-pound pork shoulder
(a.k.a. picnic or Boston butt)

1 garlic clove

2 tablespoons smoked paprika

6 tablespoons olive oil

juice of 1 orange

juice of 2 lemons

1 Stab deep slits with a knife into the pork shoulder. **2** In a small food processor or on a cutting board, make a paste from the garlic, paprika, and 2 to 3 tablespoons of the olive oil and smear it all over the pork, making sure some drips into the holes. **3** In a Dutch oven set over medium-high heat, brown the pork in the remaining olive oil. **4** Add the orange and lemon juice (about a cup of liquid total) and cover. **5** Bring to a boil, then simmer until the internal temperature of the pork is 140° F, 1½ hours.

FOR SUNDAY DINNER

Slice and serve, spooning the braising liquid over the meat and barley. (*see page 52*)

The beauty of braised meat is that it's virtually impossible to overcook. In the case of this aromatic pork recipe, a lack of attention to detail (as well as a lack of skill) are in fact rewarded by melt-off-the-bone meat. And with a 5-to-6-pound cut, you can freeze the leftovers or morph them into other meals all week long.

AND END UP WITH

LEFTOVERS

Slice and store the leftover pork in storage containers in the fridge or freezer. Freeze leftover braising liquid separately in flattened storage bags.

POSOLE

Into a medium-large pot, dump 1 29-ounce can of **hominy** (such as Goya), drained; 1 15-ounce can of **chicken broth;** 1 16-ounce jar of **tomatillo sauce;** 1 head of **romaine lettuce** (shredded); and a large chunk of leftover pork. Cook for about 10 minutes over medium-high heat, then lower to medium for another 10 minutes, allowing the pork to fall apart in the soup. Serve with sliced **radishes** and a squeeze of **lime.**

CUBAN SANDWICHES

Layer leftover pork slices, **dill pickles,** a few slices of **Swiss cheese,** and a smear of spicy **brown mustard** onto sandwich **baguettes.** Wrap them in foil and place them on a heated skillet. Place a heavy pan (cast iron is ideal) loaded down with canned items on top of the foil. Press the sandwiches until the cheese is melted, about 3 minutes.

If you don't have Swiss, you can use Gruyère, provolone, or Muenster, too.

ROASTED KABOCHA SQUASH

1 2-to-3-pound kabocha squash
(or buttercup squash or sugar pumpkin)

1 Poke a hole in the squash with a screwdriver. **2** Roast it in a shallow baking pan at 400° F for 1 hour (or 1½ hours, if it weighs closer to 3 pounds). **3** Remove, cut it open, and scrape out the seeds.

FOR SUNDAY DINNER

Scoop the squash onto plates and serve warm with butter and salt. Store leftovers in an airtight container in the fridge.

The hole jammed through the thick skin ensures that the squash won't explode in the oven. This method of cooking lets you sidestep all the carving and seed-scraping. When it's finished roasting, you can simply split it open and scoop out the seeds and flesh.

AND END UP WITH

RIGATONI *with* SQUASH

Prepare a 1-pound box of **pasta** according to the package directions, reserving the cooking water. Sauté thick slices of **onion** in **butter,** then add a few large chunks of your roasted squash. When they begin to break up (5 to 10 minutes), add the pasta with about ½ cup of **pasta water** to thin the "sauce" out. Top with **Parmesan, salt,** and **pepper.**

CHEDDAR-SQUASH MUFFINS

In a bowl, combine 2 **eggs** and ½ cup of **water** with 1 cup of squished-with-a-fork roasted squash. Then add in a 1-pound box of **oatmeal-muffin mix** (such as Dr. Oetker), ½ cup of shredded **cheddar,** and ¼ cup of chopped **scallions.** Spoon the batter into baking cups in 2 six-cup muffin tins, and bake at 400° F for 15 to 20 minutes.

CURRIED SQUASH SOUP

In a pot, combine two 15-ounce cans (or a 32-ounce box) of **chicken broth** and 2 cups of roasted squash. Add a tablespoon or so of **Indian spice** (such as garam masala, a mild curry) and heat through. Blend. Top with **cashews, raisins, sour cream,** or whatever else you'd like.

COOKED APPLES

4 apples, cored *

4 tablespoons brown sugar

1 cup apple cider

1 cinnamon stick

1 strip lemon peel

2 whole cloves

1 Peel a spiral of skin off the top of each apple, as shown. **2** Combine the remaining ingredients in a heavy medium saucepan. **3** Boil for 1 minute, then add the apples, coating them with the liquid. **4** Cover and simmer for 25 minutes, flipping the apples halfway through.

FOR SUNDAY DINNER

Slice and serve. Store leftover apples in their cooking liquid in the fridge.

* Gala, Granny Smith, and Empire are all great.

Be sure not to overcook your apples.
You want them to be soft but not mushy.

AND END UP WITH

SAUSAGE *with* APPLES

In a medium skillet over medium-high heat, brown **brats** or other **sausages** on all sides. Remove, reduce heat, and add a little **olive oil** and a medium **red onion,** ¼ head of **red cabbage,** and cooked apples (all sliced). Sauté until the cabbage wilts, about 3 minutes. Add some leftover apple liquid, along with a few tablespoons of **cider vinegar.** Turn the heat up, add the sausages back, and cook through.

APPLE PANCAKES

Remove the skin from a cooked apple and mash the flesh into pulp. Mix it into your favorite **pancake batter.** (Rule of thumb: Use ½ an apple for every 2 cups of dry mix.) Prepare pancakes according to the package directions.

APPLES *with* ICE CREAM

Reheat cooked apples in foil at 350° F for 10 minutes. Top them with a scoop of **vanilla ice cream** and a drizzle of warm **maple syrup.**

BARLEY

1 cup pearl barley

salt

1 Rinse the barley in cold water; drain. Add it to 3 cups of boiling salted water. **2** When the liquid has returned to a boil, reduce heat, cover, and simmer for 50 minutes.

FOR SUNDAY DINNER

Serve alongside the pork, drizzled with the pork's braising liquid.

(*see page 46*)

If you are the kind of person who feels naked when you eat a dinner without a starch, having a big bowl of barley in the fridge all week will be incredibly satisfying. It rounds out the plate, it's healthy, and, as evidenced by the repurposed recipes below, it's extremely versatile.

AND END UP WITH

STUFFED PEPPERS

Add 2 tablespoons of **olive oil** to a skillet set over medium heat. Sauté 1 **leek** (just the white part, cleaned and sliced), a handful of **green peas,** cooked barley, **fresh dill,** a teaspoon of **tomato paste** (or water), **salt,** and **pepper.** Stuff 4 hollowed-out bell peppers (or tomatoes) with the mixture, and bake them for 40 minutes at 375° F.

BARLEY SALAD *with* BEETS & ORANGES

Place 2 cups of cooked barley in a bowl. Toss it with cooked, peeled **beets** (available at Whole Foods); 2 sectioned **oranges;** and chopped **walnuts** or **celery** (or both). Toss with a dressing made of 1 part **orange juice** and 2 parts **olive oil.**

HOT CEREAL

Over medium-low heat, combine equal parts **milk** and cooked barley with a dash of **vanilla extract.** Cook until warmed through, about 5 minutes. Top with **dried figs, walnuts, syrup**—anything you'd put on oatmeal.

STRATEGIC SUNDAY DINNER

FLANK STEAK, GRILLED VEGETABLES & CORN BREAD

FLANK STEAK

¼ cup olive oil

6 garlic cloves, smashed

juice of 3 limes

1 tablespoon salt

pepper

2 flank steaks
(about 2 ½ pounds total)

1 In a bowl, whisk together the olive oil, garlic, lime juice, salt, and pepper. **2** Marinate your flank steaks in the mixture overnight—or for at least 2 hours—in the fridge. (Two gallon-size freezer bags are ideal for this task.) **3** Grill the steaks over high heat on a charcoal or stovetop grill, 6 to 7 minutes per side for medium-rare.

FOR SUNDAY DINNER

Reserve one steak and store it in the fridge. Let the other one rest for at least 5 minutes, then slice it (against the grain, at a slight diagonal) and serve.

The great thing about a flank steak—beyond the reasonable price tag—
is that it's so flavorful, you can stretch a very small amount of leftovers into a meal.
Each of the riffs below relies on no more than a few slices.

AND END UP WITH

SUMMER ROLLS *with* DIPPING SAUCE

Set up a bowl of warm water, a damp towel, and 8 nine-inch **rice spring-roll wrappers.** Dunk each wrapper in the water, then spread it out on the towel. Add to each a **lettuce leaf,** some shredded **carrot** and **cucumber,** several **basil** or **mint leaves,** some sliced steak, a sprinkling of **crushed peanuts,** and a squeeze of **lime.** Fold two sides into the center, then roll up to enclose the filling. For the sauce, blend ½ cup of **coconut milk,** 1 teaspoon of **soy sauce,** and ¼ cup of **peanut butter.**

MEXICAN STEAK & EGGS

Heat a cup of chopped steak in a couple of tablespoons of **olive oil** over medium-high heat for 3 minutes. Reduce heat to medium and add a cup of jarred **pico de gallo** and 4 beaten **eggs.** Cook, turning with a spatula, until the eggs are set, about 5 minutes. Serve with warm **tortillas** and a squeeze of **lime.**

CUBAN SLOPPY JOES

In a large skillet over medium heat, combine 2 cups each of chopped steak and **grilled vegetables** (*see the following page*) with 2 tablespoons each of chopped **raisins** and **green olives,** ½ cup each of **ketchup** and **water,** a tablespoon of **Worcestershire sauce,** 1 teaspoon each of **chili powder** and **cumin,** and ¼ teaspoon of **allspice.** Cook, stirring, until most of the liquid has evaporated, about 15 minutes. Serve on **rolls** with **plantain chips.**

Great for the lunchbox!

GRILLED VEGETABLES

½ cup olive oil

2 tablespoons fresh oregano

1 tablespoon salt

6 garlic cloves, chopped

3 onions, peeled and sliced into thick rounds

4 tomatoes, halved

4 red bell peppers, membranes and stems removed, and quartered

1 green bell pepper, membranes and stems removed, and quartered

6 ears corn, husked

1 In a large bowl, whisk the olive oil with the oregano, salt, and garlic; toss with the vegetables and set aside for 1 hour. **2** Grill everything over medium-high heat for 5 to 7 minutes on each side, turning once. Don't worry if the pepper skins turn black and blistered—the flesh will still be good. Scrape off any large black parts before serving.

FOR SUNDAY DINNER
Reserve the green pepper, a few slices of red pepper, and the kernels scraped from 2 ears of corn in zipper bags in the fridge for use in the other recipes. Serve the rest on a platter, sprinkled with sherry vinegar.

On every kitchen counter in Spain, you'll find a huge jar of cooked peppers, onions, and tomatoes. It's the base for all their (and now your) dinner needs.

PASTA & BEAN SOUP

In a large pot, fry 3 **garlic cloves** in ⅓ cup of **olive oil** until they begin to brown. Discard the garlic and add a chopped **zucchini** and a tablespoon of **tomato paste.** Cook for 1 minute. Puree 2 cups of grilled vegetables and add them to the pot with a 15-ounce can of **cannellini beans** and a quart of **chicken broth.** Bring to a boil, then add ½ cup of **ditalini pasta.** Cover and simmer until the pasta is tender, 10 to 12 minutes.

CHICKEN PAPRIKASH

In a large pan, sauté 2 pounds of bone-in **chicken pieces** until they're browned on all sides, about 5 minutes. Add 2 cups of chopped grilled vegetables, a tablespoon each of **tomato paste** and **paprika, 2 bay leaves,** ½ cup of **water,** and **salt** and **pepper** to taste. Reduce heat and simmer, covered, for about 20 minutes. Stir in ½ cup of **sour cream,** and serve with **egg noodles** or **corkscrew pasta.**

JAMBALAYA

Sauté a pound of chunked boneless, skinless **chicken thighs** in **olive oil** with 2 sliced mild **red-pepper sausages** and 2 chopped **celery stalks** until the meat is opaque, about 4 minutes. Add a cup of raw **white rice** and a teaspoon each of **salt** and **Creole** or **Old Bay seasoning.** Cook for 1 minute, then add a **bay leaf** and 2 cups each of chopped grilled vegetables and **chicken broth.** Bring to a boil, then reduce heat and simmer, covered, for 20 minutes or until the rice is tender.

CORN BREAD

2 eggs

¼ cup vegetable oil

¼ cup sugar

1 cup plain yogurt

1 cup all-purpose flour

1 cup stone-ground cornmeal

½ teaspoon baking soda

½ teaspoon salt

2 teaspoons baking powder

1 Grease an 8-inch cast-iron skillet (or a cornbread mold if you have one) and place it on a heated, covered grill. **2** In a large bowl, whisk together the eggs, vegetable oil, sugar, and yogurt. **3** In a second bowl, combine the flour, cornmeal, baking soda, salt, and baking powder. **4** Add the dry ingredients to the wet ones in two batches, stirring until just combined. **5** Fill the pan with half of the batter. (Refrigerate the other half for leftover riffs at right.) **6** Cook it on the grill, covered, for 10 to 12 minutes.

FOR SUNDAY DINNER

Slice and serve hot from the pan. Store leftovers on the counter, in an airtight container.

Time to use that sack of cornmeal more creatively. Here, three I-would-never-have-thought-of-that! riffs on regular old corn bread and its batter.

CORN GRIDDLE CAKES

Add the following to a half batch (about 1 cup) of corn-bread batter: ½ cup each of reserved **grilled corn** and diced **red pepper** *(see page 58)*, ½ cup of shredded **mozzarella,** and a dash of **chile powder.** Drop the mixture by tablespoonfuls onto the hot griddle, turning once, and cook until browned, 2 minutes per side. Serve with **guacamole** or **sour cream.**

OVEN-FRIED CATFISH

Preheat oven to 425° F. Lightly grease a baking sheet and place 4 six-ounce **catfish fillets** on it. In a bowl, mix ½ cup of **plain yogurt** with a teaspoon each of **salt** and **Creole** or **Old Bay seasoning.** Spread the fish with the yogurt mixture, press a generous amount of stale (or toasted) corn-bread crumbs into it, and bake for 8 to 12 minutes.

VEGETABLE PAKORAS

In a large pot over medium heat, warm 2 inches of **vegetable oil.** Add the following to a half batch (about 1 cup) of corn-bread batter: 2 teaspoons of **garam masala,** a teaspoon of **salt,** and ½ cup of **shredded coconut.** Stir in 4 cups of roughly chopped **vegetables** (such as **broccoli, cauliflower, carrots,** or **string beans**). Fry tablespoons of the mixture until crisp, about a minute. Drain on paper towels and serve with **chutney** or **yogurt.**

8 THINGS TO DO ON THE WEEKEND TO GET AHEAD FOR THE WEEK

Even those of us who like to spend time in the kitchen find our patience compromised during the general joy-suck that is weeknight cooking. To combat this, we find that taking the time to do a few small prep tasks on Sunday, when we may actually have a little breathing room, helps tremendously. Try any of the eight tasks on the following pages—as simple as washing lettuce, as ambitious as making a marinara— and you'll be two steps ahead for getting dinner on the table all week long.

When your "nesting instinct" kicks in at 35 weeks, this is the sauce you'll want to cook up and stash away like a maniac.

NUMBER 1

MAKE A MARINARA

⅓ cup olive oil

4 garlic cloves, smashed

2 28-ounce cans whole tomatoes
(preferably San Marzano)
with their juices

salt

6 to 7 basil leaves *(optional)*

1 Cover the bottom of a large, shallow, straight-sided pan with the olive oil. (Olive oil takes a marinara from good to great. Use more than you think you need.) **2** Over low heat, sauté the garlic until fragrant. Add the tomatoes and their juices, squishing them with your hands as you go. **3** Add the salt and basil (if using). Cook over low heat for 15 to 20 minutes.

YOU'LL BE TWO STEPS AHEAD FOR

MEATBALL SANDWICHES *(see page 219)*

TOMATO & BEAN SOUP Blend 3 cups of marinara with 1 cup of chicken broth and add some cooked rice or beans.

PERSONAL-PAN LASAGNAS *(see page 155)*

Freeze flat in large zipper bags so it takes less time to thaw when you need it.

64

They're cheap and high in protein, and the dried kinds can be stored forever. Do what the rest of the planet does—make them a weekly staple.

BOIL A POT OF BEANS

1 pound dry beans (*such as white, black, red, garbanzo*)

baking soda

1 Soak your beans in water and a generous pinch of baking soda overnight. **2** Cover them with water (by a few inches) in a medium pan and bring it to a boil. Boil for 1 minute. **3** Remove from heat, cover, and set aside for 1 hour.

YOU'LL BE TWO STEPS AHEAD FOR

RICE & BEANS Combine black beans with sautéed onions, peppers, garlic, tomatoes, and cooked rice.

PASTA E FAGIOLI Mix white beans and small-shaped pasta, such as alphabet shapes, into a store-bought carton of tomato soup.

CROSTINI Combine white beans with a can of tuna; a bit of sage, tarragon, or rosemary; and a squeeze of lemon. Serve on sliced baguette toasts.

Your search for the perfect roast chicken recipe is over.
It's almost impossible to mess this one up.

ROAST A CHICKEN

1 4-pound chicken

2 tablespoons unsalted butter, softened

salt and pepper

1 lemon, pricked several times with a sharp knife

1 small bunch fresh thyme

½ head garlic, sliced as shown

1 Preheat oven to 450° F. **2** Rinse the chicken and pat it dry. Rub the skin with the butter and season it with salt and pepper. Fill the cavity with the lemon, thyme, and garlic. Cross the legs and tie them firmly with butcher twine. Place the chicken breast-side up in a roasting pan. **3** Roast until the internal temperature in the thickest part of the thigh reads 165° F, about 1 hour, 15 minutes. Allow the chicken to rest for 15 minutes before carving.

YOU'LL BE TWO STEPS AHEAD FOR

SLICED-CHICKEN SANDWICHES
On a crusty baguette with cole slaw and mustard.

TORTILLA SOUP, COUNTRY-CLUB CHICKEN SALAD & POTPIES WITH BISCUITS *(see page 228)*

Twisted strips of foil work in place of twine.

Once you have a batch of this around, you'll become evangelical about its transformative powers.

CARAMELIZE SOME ONIONS

4 medium-large onions, sliced or chopped

4 tablespoons olive oil

salt and pepper

1 Over low heat, sauté the onions in the olive oil. Add a generous pinch of salt and a few grinds of pepper. **2** Stir occasionally, allowing the onions to cook down for 30 to 45 minutes, or as long as you have. They freeze quite nicely in storage bags.

YOU'LL BE TWO STEPS AHEAD FOR

BAKED-POTATO DINNER Pile up baked potatoes with the onions and any of the traditional toppings: spinach, cheese, bacon, sour cream.

PASTA WITH PARMESAN & ONIONS Cook ribbon pasta according to the package directions, toss it with olive oil, and sprinkle it generously with Parmesan and caramelized onions.

ALMOST ANYTHING A heap of these elevate the simplest dishes— eggs, burgers, potato salads, pastas…

Yes, there are hundreds of bottled dressing options. But this supereasy homemade vinaigrette makes everything it touches taste brighter.

NUMBER 5

MAKE A VINAIGRETTE

¼ cup white-wine
or red-wine vinegar

¾ cup olive oil

1 heaping tablespoon
minced shallots

1 teaspoon mustard

salt and pepper

1 In a small mixing bowl, whisk together all the ingredients. **2** Transfer the mixture to a jar and store it in the refrigerator for up to 2 weeks. You can also add the ingredients directly to the jar, then shake.

YOU'LL BE TWO STEPS AHEAD FOR

CLASSIC COBB SALAD *(see page 152)*

MAYO-PHOBE'S POTATO SALAD Boil peeled Yukon gold potatoes for 15 minutes, toss them with the dressing while still warm, and add any herbs you have on hand.

ANY FAVORITE SALAD Whether it's lettuce-based, rice-based, quinoa-based, or barley-based, a drizzle of this will make it come alive.

If you find yourself avoiding vegetables that require a blanch, steam, chop, and wash, this will make life easier.

WASH GREENS & BLANCH VEGETABLES

1 or more bunches vegetables and/or herbs, such as broccoli, green beans, asparagus, cauliflower, brussels sprouts, basil, cilantro, dill, and parsley

Wash and store the greens and herbs, and steam or blanch the broccoli, beans, asparagus, cauliflower, brussels sprouts, or other vegetable.

YOU'LL BE TWO STEPS AHEAD FOR

SALADS Corn & Shrimp Salad *(see page 207)*, Country-Club Chicken Salad *(see page 229)*, Stone-Fruit Salad. *(see page 223)*

STIR-FRIES Including Seared Tofu *with* Pork & Broccoli. *(see page 231)*

VEGETABLE FRITTERS *(see page 235)*

Whatever herbs you don't use up can be dried by microwaving for a minute.

We call this a chili blend, but if your child likes it enough, label the jar "[Kid's name]'s special spice."

MIX A CHILI BLEND

1 ½ teaspoons toasted cumin seeds

1 teaspoon garlic powder

1 dried ancho chile, stemmed and seeded

1 teaspoon oregano

½ teaspoon cinnamon

¼ teaspoon ground cloves

2 tablespoons unsweetened cocoa

1 Combine all the ingredients and store in an airtight jar away from heat and light.

YOU'LL BE TWO STEPS AHEAD FOR

BASIC CHILI Sauté a handful of chopped onions and a minced garlic clove. Add a pound of ground meat, salt, and pepper. Mix in two small cans of tomato sauce, 4 tablespoons of the chili blend, and ½ teaspoon of cayenne (if desired). Simmer for 20 minutes.

SPICY SALMON Rub the blend on some salmon fillets. Sear them in a little olive oil over medium heat for 5 minutes per side.

CUBAN SLOPPY JOES *(see page 57)*

These basic flavor-building blocks—garlic, onion, ginger—turn into one building block . . . literally.

NUMBER 8

FREEZE GINGER-GARLIC-ONION CUBES

3 tablespoons olive oil

1 hand-size piece ginger, peeled and minced

1 head garlic, peeled and minced

1 large onion, peeled and chopped

1 In the olive oil, sauté the ginger, garlic, and onion. **2** In a small food processor, blend the mixture with 1 teaspoon of water. **3** Freeze the mixture in an ice-cube tray and, once frozen, store the cubes in zipper bags. Thaw cubes inside the bag under running water, or just add them directly to your hot pan when it's time to cook. Each cube equals about 2 tablespoons.

YOU'LL BE TWO STEPS AHEAD FOR

HALIBUT, CHICKPEA & SQUASH STEW Use 3 to 4 cubes.
(see page 114)

ONE-POT COCONUT-CHICKEN CURRY Use 3 cubes.
(see page 88)

I WANT SOMETHING SIMPLE, FAST, AND HARD TO SCREW UP

DINNERS TO FALL BACK ON AGAIN AND AGAIN

Not every night is a mad scramble of blood, sweat, and tears (yours and/or theirs). Some are actually…normal. Well, sort of. That is, once you accept the fact that on any given evening, ballet class may run late, your neighbor may corner you during a "quick" stop for milk, and your baby may spiral into the witching hour once you walk in the door. For your newly recalibrated "normal," we have assembled quick (30 minutes or less), healthy, repertoire-worthy dinners that have been hand-picked to cater to parents' everyday lives.

Repeat after us: IT'S NOT CHAOTIC. IT'S RICH.

Here, sturdy lettuce leaves do the work of traditional dumpling wrappers. If that's not an easy enough sell, the dipping sauce will be.

active time: 20 minutes
total time: 30 minutes
serves: 4

sweet pork hand rolls

1½ garlic cloves, minced

1 tablespoon olive oil

¾ pound ground pork

1 teaspoon Chinese five-spice powder

2 tablespoons brown sugar

3 tablespoons soy sauce

8 to 10 sturdy Bibb or Romaine lettuce leaves

1 carrot, shredded

1 cucumber, peeled and julienned

chopped peanuts

2 tablespoons sugar

4 tablespoons lime juice

1   In a skillet over medium-low heat, cook 1 clove of the garlic in the oil until fragrant, about 2 minutes.

2   Add the pork, five-spice powder, brown sugar, and 1 tablespoon of the soy sauce. Raise heat to high and cook until the pork is browned, 8 to 10 minutes.

3   Scoop the pork mixture into the lettuce leaves. Garnish with the carrot, cucumber, and peanuts.

4   Combine the sugar and lime juice with the remaining garlic and soy sauce to make the dipping sauce.

Works great with ground turkey, too.

We recommend making this in late summer, when tomatoes are in season. For those few weeks, you'll want to serve it to the family for every meal. (And there's really no reason you shouldn't.)

active time: 10 minutes
total time: 15 minutes
serves: 4

spaghetti *with* hand-crushed tomatoes

8 ounces thin spaghetti

2 pints cherry tomatoes
(*orange, red, yellow, teardrop—whatever*)

2 garlic cloves, peeled and finely chopped

4 tablespoons extra-virgin olive oil

6 to 7 basil leaves, torn

1 cup fresh arugula (*optional*)

salt and pepper

1 Cook the pasta al dente.

2 Meanwhile, in a large bowl, squeeze the tomatoes to break them up.

3 Add the garlic, oil, basil, arugula (if using), salt, and pepper; set aside.

4 Drain the pasta (reserving ½ cup of the water) and toss it with the tomatoes. If the pasta is still a little dry, add some of the cooking water.

5 Let sit until the heat from the pasta has cooked the tomatoes and garlic slightly and wilted the arugula, 1 to 2 minutes. Serve warm or at room temperature.

Put the kids in charge of smushing the tomatoes here.

Quick grits are the way to go here. They're ready in 5 minutes and require minimal attention.

active time: 30 minutes
total time: 45 minutes
serves: 4

shrimp & grits

6 slices smoky bacon, chopped

2 garlic cloves, peeled and smashed

1 medium onion, chopped

1 stalk celery, chopped

½ red bell pepper, chopped

½ green bell pepper, chopped

1 tablespoon tomato paste

1½ teaspoons Old Bay seasoning

½ teaspoon smoked paprika

1 15-ounce can diced tomatoes

¾ cup quick grits

¾ pound large shrimp, peeled

1 In a large skillet over medium-high heat, fry the bacon for about 5 minutes. Reduce heat slightly, add the garlic and vegetables, and cook, stirring, for another 10 minutes.

2 Add the tomato paste, Old Bay, and paprika. Stir and cook for 1 minute, then add the tomatoes.

3 Increase heat to medium. Cover and simmer for 10 minutes.

4 Prepare the grits according to the package instructions.

5 Uncover the skillet and add the shrimp. Stir and cover, then cook until the shrimp is opaque and cooked, another few minutes. Serve over the grits.

A parent, more than anyone, can appreciate a recipe that works overtime. Here, the minty marinade does double duty as a dip.

active time: 15 minutes
total time: 20 minutes
serves: 4

loin lamb chops *with* minted yogurt*

leaves from 1 bunch mint, cleaned

3 garlic cloves, peeled

⅓ cup olive oil

3 tablespoons balsamic vinegar

1 teaspoon salt

1 cup plain yogurt
(preferably Greek)

6 loin lamb chops
(about 1½ pounds total)

1   Heat the grill (charcoal or stovetop).

2   In a blender, mix everything but the lamb and the yogurt. Combine half that mixture with the yogurt. Slather the other half on the meat.

3   Grill the lamb chops for about 4 minutes each side. Serve with the yogurt mixture and a side of cooked carrots.

*or ketchup

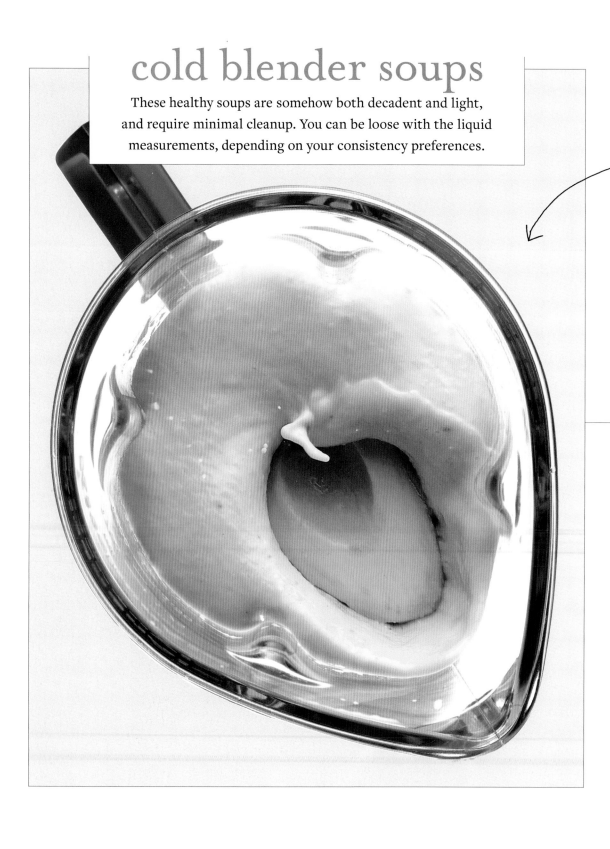

cold blender soups

These healthy soups are somehow both decadent and light, and require minimal cleanup. You can be loose with the liquid measurements, depending on your consistency preferences.

buttermilk-avocado soup

active time: 10 minutes | *total time:* 10 minutes to 1 hour (*if chilled*) | *makes:* 2 bowls

1 ripe avocado

½ small shallot,
roughly chopped

juice of ½ lemon

1 cup buttermilk

1 large seedless cucumber,
peeled and cut into chunks

1 pinch cumin

1 Blend together all the ingredients until liquefied. **2** Serve with a dollop of sour cream.

pinkalicious borscht

active time: 10 minutes | *total time:* 10 minutes to 1 hour (*if chilled*) | *makes:* 2 bowls

8 ounces precooked beets
(*about 2*), cut into chunks

1¾ cups chicken broth

juice of ½ lemon

1 tablespoon roughly chopped
shallots

1 pinch salt

1 pinch sugar

1 Put all the ingredients in the blender and process until smooth. **2** Serve immediately with
a dollop of sour cream, or chill for later.

cucumber-yogurt soup

active time: 10 minutes | *total time:* 10 minutes to 1 hour (*if chilled*) | *makes:* 2 bowls

1 garlic clove

1 large seedless cucumber (*or
1½ regular cucumbers, seeded*),
peeled and cut into large chunks

8 ounces plain yogurt (*use
Greek yogurt for a thicker soup*)

1 to 2 teaspoons sherry vinegar

2 tablespoons chopped
fresh dill

salt and pepper

1 Use a garlic press to crush the garlic directly into the blender. **2** Add the other ingredients
and blend until well combined. **3** Serve immediately or chill for later.

Try adding cooked shrimp to the avocado or cucumber soup.

We love this meal because chucking the lima beans into the boiling pasta water means one less pot to clean.

active time: 20 minutes
total time: 20 minutes
serves: 4

wagon-wheel pasta & goat cheese

½ **pound wagon-wheel** (*or any short*) **pasta**

1 10-ounce box frozen lima beans, thawed

1 tablespoon olive oil

1 large onion, sliced thinly

2 tablespoons sour cream (*or crème fraîche*)

1 tablespoon finely chopped fresh thyme (*optional*)

½ **teaspoon salt**

¼ **teaspoon pepper**

4 ounces creamy aged goat cheese, cut into small chunks

1   Bring a large pot of salted water to a boil, then add the pasta.

2   After 5 minutes, add the lima beans.

3   Meanwhile, heat the olive oil in a skillet over medium heat. Add the onion and cook until browned, about 7 minutes. Set aside.

4   When the pasta is ready, drain it with the beans (reserving ½ cup of the liquid), then return the pasta and beans to the pot along with the onion, sour cream or crème fraîche, thyme (if using), salt, pepper, and the reserved water. Add the goat cheese, toss together, and serve. (For a creamier sauce, add the goat cheese *before* the water rather than after.)

You can use edamame or peas in place of the lima beans.

Madras curry powder is a nice starter curry for kids—it's mild but still has a good range of flavors.

active time: 25 minutes
total time: 30 minutes
serves: 4

one-pot coconut-chicken curry

1 pound chicken tenders
(*preferably kosher*)

salt

3 tablespoons vegetable oil

1 small onion, peeled and chopped

1 garlic clove, peeled

1 tablespoon grated fresh ginger

2 tablespoons madras curry powder

½ teaspoon ground coriander

¼ teaspoon ground cumin

1 cup chicken broth

1 cup coconut milk

1 large Granny Smith apple, cut into small chunks

ASSORTED TOPPINGS
roasted cashews or peanuts, fresh mango chunks, toasted coconut, chopped scallions, raisins

1   Season the chicken with the salt; set aside. Over medium-high heat, warm the oil in a wide, shallow saucepan or small Dutch oven.

2   Sauté the onion, garlic, and ginger for 2 minutes. Add the curry powder, coriander, and cumin and cook, stirring, until fragrant, another minute or two.

3   Add the broth and coconut milk and simmer for 10 minutes to thicken. Add the chicken and apple and cook for an additional 10 minutes or until cooked through. Serve with rice and whatever toppings you like.

Serve this with rice that has been drenched in melted garlic butter. It's not exactly heart-healthy, but if ever there was a recipe to convince a kid to eat fish…

active time: 10 minutes
total time: 30 minutes
serves: 4

bacon-wrapped fish nuggets

1 garlic clove, halved

1 bunch scallions, trimmed and halved lengthwise (*optional*)

2 pounds cod fillets, cut into nugget-size chunks

salt and pepper

16 strips bacon

1   Preheat oven to 475° F.

2   Place the garlic and scallions (if using) on a baking sheet.

3   Season the fish with the salt and pepper and wrap each piece in the bacon, trimming the strips as necessary.

4   Roast in the lower third of the oven for 20 minutes or until the fish flakes easily.

This dish is a boon for any parent who has to deal with forcing a skinny-Minnie toddler to gain weight. The mustard cuts the richness of the cream, so it feels like an elegant everyday meal for the rest of the family, too.

active time: 15 minutes
total time: 20 minutes
serves: 4

creamy chicken *with* shallots

½ cup all-purpose flour

½ teaspoon paprika

salt and pepper

4 chicken-breast cutlets
(about 6 ounces each)

2 tablespoons vegetable oil

1 large shallot, diced

½ cup white wine
(or chicken broth)

½ cup heavy cream

1 teaspoon Dijon mustard

1 Season the flour with the paprika, salt, and pepper. Coat the chicken cutlets in the flour, shaking off the excess.

2 Heat the oil in a large, heavy-bottomed saucepan over medium-high heat and sauté the chicken in two batches, turning once, until browned, about 2 minutes on each side. Transfer it to a plate. In the same pan, sauté the shallot until browned, about 5 minutes.

3 Add the wine or broth and boil until reduced by half, about 2 minutes. Add the cream and mustard and return to a boil.

4 Reduce heat to medium and return the chicken and its juices to the skillet. Continue to cook until the cream is reduced and coating the breasts, turning once, another 7 to 9 minutes. Serve with steamed peas.

This is the ultimate
in-a-pinch meal.
It's easy to make, and
it's easy to keep the
ingredients on hand.

active time: 15 minutes
total time: 15 minutes
serves: 4

beans & toast

4 thick slices country bread

4 tablespoons olive oil

2 garlic cloves, peeled and sliced

a few fresh sage leaves

1 28-ounce can diced tomatoes

1 15-ounce can cannellini beans, drained

½ teaspoon salt

¼ teaspoon pepper

1   Sprinkle the bread with 2 tablespoons of the oil. Toast the slices until crusty and golden.

2   Heat the remaining oil in a large skillet, then add the garlic and sage and stir until the garlic begins to brown, about 1 minute.

3   Add the tomatoes, beans, salt, and pepper and stir to combine. Cook over medium-high heat until the liquid is reduced and slightly thickened, a few more minutes.

4   Serve, placing a slice of toast into each soup bowl and generously spooning the beans and broth right over the bread, if the kids will let you.

The speed of this recipe relies on cooked rice.
Look for precooked rice at the store, or make
a mental note from this point forward to always
save the leftover rice from Chinese takeout.

active time: 15 minutes
total time: 25 minutes
serves: 4

bibimbap

¾ cup soy sauce

6 tablespoons toasted sesame oil

4 tablespoons light brown sugar

1 pound ground turkey, beef, or pork

2 tablespoons vegetable oil

4 large eggs

2 cups cooked rice

assorted steamed or raw vegetables (*shredded carrot, canned baby corn, spinach, bean sprouts, red onion…*)

toasted sesame seeds

1   Mix together the soy sauce, sesame oil, and brown sugar; set aside.

2   In a pan, brown the meat in 1 tablespoon of the vegetable oil, about 5 minutes. Add half the soy-sauce mixture and continue cooking until the liquid is absorbed, 3 to 4 minutes. Remove from heat and cover.

3   In another pan, fry the eggs in the remaining vegetable oil, 4 to 5 minutes.

4   Divide the rice among 4 bowls. Arrange some vegetables and meat and an egg in each. Sprinkle with the sesame seeds, then drizzle the remaining soy-sauce mixture over the top.

Highly customizable for picky eaters.

Who would have thought that a juice box would provide poaching liquid with just the right balance of sweet and tangy?

active time: 5 minutes
total time: 20 minutes
serves: 4

juice-box salmon

1 juice-box lemonade
(8 ounces)

salt and white pepper

**1 pound salmon fillets,
skin on, cut into 4 pieces**

**2 tablespoons Russian
dressing or to taste**

1   Preheat oven to 500° F.

2   Pour the lemonade into a 9-by-12-inch baking dish.

3   Salt and pepper the salmon and place it in a pan, skin-side down. Lay a piece of parchment or foil loosely on top and roast it for 15 minutes.

4   Plate the salmon and tent it with foil. Pour the liquid into a saucepan. Boil until syrupy, about 10 to 15 minutes, then drizzle it over the salmon. Serve the kids' salmon with Russian dressing on the side.

What's not to love about a sauce that you throw in the blender and is done in 3 seconds?

active time: 15 minutes
total time: 15 minutes
serves: 4

grilled skirt steak *with* blender chimichurri

4 garlic cloves, peeled

½ cup olive oil

1 teaspoon salt

1 tablespoon dried oregano

2 pieces skirt steak
(*about 1 pound*)

leaves from 1 bunch
Italian parsley

¼ cup red-wine vinegar

¼ teaspoon crushed red-pepper flakes (*optional*)

1   Heat a grill (or a heavy skillet) to medium-high.

2   In a blender, combine the garlic, olive oil, salt, and oregano until smooth. Remove a couple of tablespoons of the mixture and slather it all over the steak. Add the parsley, vinegar, and pepper flakes (if using) and blend until almost smooth.

3   Cook the meat, turning once, until browned, 3 to 4 minutes on each side. Serve with the chimichurri sauce.

The tiny chunks of meat, fruit, and veggies are kid-friendly, but the tart pomegranate mixed with sweet plums make the dish dinner-party-worthy.

active time: 30 minutes
total time: 30 minutes
serves: 4

sweet & sour chicken *with* plums

2 tablespoons cornstarch

⅓ cup sugar

¼ cup white distilled vinegar

½ cup pomegranate juice
(or pineapple juice)

3 tablespoons soy sauce

2 teaspoons vegetable oil

3 unpeeled firm, sweet plums, cut into chunks

1 large stalk celery, sliced

1 bunch scallions, trimmed and cut into 1-inch lengths

2 garlic cloves, minced

1½ pounds boneless, skinless chicken thighs, cut into small cubes

¼ teaspoon Chinese five-spice powder

salt and pepper

1   In a small bowl, whisk together the cornstarch, sugar, vinegar, pomegranate or pineapple juice, and soy sauce; set aside.

2   Heat the oil in a wok or large skillet over medium-high heat. Add the plums, celery, and scallions and cook for 2 minutes. Add the garlic and cook for 1 minute, then add the chicken, five-spice powder, salt, and pepper.

3   Stir and cook until the chicken is beginning to brown, another 3 to 4 minutes. Reduce heat and add the sauce. Stir until it thickens, another minute or so. Serve with steamed rice.

Once you get your kids to like meatballs, a whole world will open up. This version is particularly exciting. Wet your hands when shaping the meatballs to prevent sticking.

active time: 30 minutes
total time: 30 minutes
serves: 4 to 6

Swedish meatballs

1 pound ground beef

¾ cup bread crumbs, combined with ½ cup milk

1 egg

1 teaspoon salt

¼ teaspoon pepper

1 small onion, finely chopped

½ teaspoon ground allspice

¼ teaspoon grated nutmeg

4 tablespoons unsalted butter

4½ teaspoons all-purpose flour

1 cup chicken broth

½ cup sour cream

lingonberry or cranberry sauce (*optional*)

1 Combine the beef, bread crumbs, egg, salt, pepper, onion, allspice, and nutmeg. Using your hands, form the mixture into 1-inch balls.

2 Place 3 tablespoons of the butter in a skillet over medium-high heat. Brown the meatballs for about 10 minutes.

3 Remove them and most of the fat; set the meatballs aside. Stir the flour and the remaining butter into the pan.

4 Add the broth. Simmer until it thickens, about 2 minutes.

5 Strain the mixture with a sieve to remove clumps. Return it to the pan.

6 Reduce heat to low and stir in the sour cream. Return the meatballs to the pan for 1 minute. Serve with the berry sauce (if using).

Gremolata sounds fancy, and actually...it is.
(Don't you crave an upgrade from chicken and
potatoes?) You'll find yourself committing
this one to memory and cooking it on autopilot.

active time: 20 minutes
total time: 30 minutes
serves: 4

lemony chicken *with* potatoes & gremolata

4 tablespoons olive oil

4 boneless, skinless chicken breasts *(about 1½ pounds)*, cut into 1½-inch pieces

2 garlic cloves, peeled and halved

1 small onion, peeled and chopped

6 smallish new potatoes, scrubbed and quartered

salt and pepper

½ cup chicken broth *(or water)*

juice of 2 lemons

GREMOLATA

zest of 2 lemons

1 small handful Italian parsley

1 garlic clove, peeled

salt

1   In a large skillet over medium-high heat, heat half the oil and brown the chicken with the garlic, turning it a few times, about 8 minutes. Remove all of it (including the garlic) to a large bowl.

2   Add the remaining oil to the pan and brown the onion and potatoes, about 8 minutes. Season generously with the salt and pepper. (Potatoes absorb more seasoning than you think.)

3   Add the broth or water and juice (zest the lemons for the gremolata before juicing), and increase heat for about a minute, scraping up the brown bits in the pan. Return the chicken and its juices to the skillet. Cover, reduce heat to medium, and continue to cook until the potatoes are tender and the liquid has thickened, another 15 minutes.

4   Meanwhile, make the gremolata: On a cutting board, chop all the ingredients together finely but not too finely. Sprinkle the mixture over the chicken and potatoes just before serving.

VERY SIMPLE, VERY USEFUL BROWN-AND-BRAISE TECHNIQUE

① Brown meat in oil. Remove.
② Add onions, veggies, and dried/fresh herbs to the same pan.
③ Add meat back to pan with liquid (wine or stock).
     Raise heat, then simmer until the meat is cooked through.
④ Voila!

This definitely takes a little longer to cook than a typical weeknight meal. So make it on Sunday and reheat it for 30 minutes at 350° F on Monday.

active time: 15 minutes
total time: 1 hour, 15 minutes
serves: 8 to 10

rigatoni casserole *with* tofu

¼ cup olive oil, plus more for drizzling

½ onion, finely chopped

2 garlic cloves, finely chopped

1 28-ounce can crushed tomatoes

1 teaspoon dried oregano

1 12- or 14-ounce package firm tofu, drained

1 large egg

1 pinch grated nutmeg

salt and pepper

1 10-ounce package frozen spinach, defrosted and drained

1 1-pound box rigatoni, cooked al dente and drained

1 pound fresh mozzarella, grated (*about 4 cups*)

3 ounces grated Parmesan (*about ¾ cup*)

1   Preheat oven to 350° F.

2   Heat the oil in a saucepan over medium-high heat. Add the onion. Sauté for 3 minutes, then add the garlic and cook until the onion is translucent, about 2 minutes more.

3   Add the tomatoes and oregano. Reduce heat and simmer, stirring occasionally, for 15 minutes. Meanwhile, in a blender, process the tofu, egg, nutmeg, salt, and pepper until smooth.

4   Transfer the mixture to a bowl and fold in the spinach, cooked rigatoni, tomato sauce, 1 cup of the mozzarella, and ½ cup of the Parmesan.

5   Drizzle a coating of olive oil into a 9-by-13-inch baking pan. Add the pasta mixture and sprinkle the remaining cheeses over the top. Bake until golden and bubbling, 35 to 40 minutes. Let cool for 10 minutes before slicing (or refrigerating).

If the litmus test for a good kids' meal that grown-ups will like is "Can I serve this with a glass of wine?" then this one is great.

active time: 10 minutes
total time: 25 minutes
serves: 4

tomato egg cup

4 medium vine-ripened
tomatoes

salt and pepper

4 large eggs

4 tablespoons shredded
white cheddar cheese

4 slices toast, cut into strips
(as shown)

1   Preheat oven to 425° F.

2   Slice off and set aside the top third of each tomato.
    Scoop out the seeds.

3   Place the tomatoes in a glass or ceramic baking dish.
    Season with the salt and pepper.

4   Break an egg into each tomato.

5   Bake, with the sliced tops set beside them, for 15 minutes.

6   Top the tomatoes with the cheese and bake until
    the cheese is bubbly, 5 to 7 minutes more.

7   Let cool for 5 minutes. Serve with the tops and toast
    strips for dipping.

Your child will be delighted to know that the toasts are called "soldiers."

restaurant replication

Wouldn't it be nice if your kids approached dinner at your
house with the same gusto that they do at the local pizza joint?
These three homemade kid-menu VIPs attempt to replicate
the dining experience at home in as healthy a way as possible.

chicken fingers

1½ pounds organic boneless chicken breasts

2 eggs, beaten

½ cup all-purpose flour

salt and pepper

1¼ cups cornflake crumbs

1 Pound the living hell out of your chicken. (Do not bother continuing with this recipe if you skip this step. It is by far the most important.) Cut it into strips that resemble the size and shape of the chicken fingers at your kids' favorite restaurant. 2 Set up your dredging stations: a rimmed plate with the eggs, a plate with the mound of flour (salted and peppered), and a plate with the cornflake crumbs. 3 Dredge your pounded chicken pieces first in the flour, then in the egg, then in the crumbs. 4 Sauté them in olive oil over medium-high heat for about 2 to 3 minutes a side. Serve hot with a great big dollop of ketchup.

salmon teriyaki

¼ cup soy sauce

¼ cup sake

⅓ cup mirin
(*Japanese sweet wine*)

1 tablespoon sugar

1 pound wild-salmon filet

1 Combine all the ingredients but the salmon in a small saucepan and bring them to a boil. Reduce heat to moderately low and simmer until reduced by about a third, about 15 minutes. Pour the mixture into a shallow bowl and let cool for about 10 minutes. 2 Broil the salmon on a foil-lined baking sheet for 15 minutes, brushing the glaze on every 4 to 5 minutes as it cooks. Serve with rice, steamed carrot chunks, and broccoli.

popcorn shrimp

¾ cup vegetable oil

½ cup flour

1 cup club soda

1 pinch each salt and pepper

1 cup panko crumbs

2 tablespoons fresh oregano
(*or 2 teaspoons dry*)

1 pound shrimp, peeled

1 Add the oil to a large skillet over medium-high heat. (It should be about ¼ inch deep.) 2 In a bowl, mix together the flour, club soda, salt, and pepper. 3 On a plate, combine the panko crumbs and oregano. 4 Dredge the shrimp in the flour mixture, then in the panko crumbs. Fry them in the pan until cooked through, 1 to 2 minutes a side each. Drain on paper towels and serve.

The fish gets hidden among all the brothy goodness and may very well go undetected by the finger-poking police.

active time: 15 minutes
total time: 45 minutes✳
serves: 4

halibut, chickpea & squash stew

1 onion, chopped

4 garlic cloves, peeled and halved

1 3-inch chunk unpeeled ginger, sliced

4 tablespoons unsalted butter

1 bunch cilantro, including stems (*you'll fish them out later*)

1 pinch saffron

1 teaspoon garam masala

4 cups chicken broth

1 15-ounce can chickpeas, drained

1 1-pound butternut squash, peeled and chopped into large pieces

1 zucchini, chopped

1 pound tilapia or halibut, cut into large chunks

2 cups uncooked couscous, in a heatproof serving bowl

1   In a large pot over medium-high heat, sauté the onion, garlic, and ginger in the butter for about 5 minutes.

2   Add the remaining ingredients except a few stems of cilantro, the fish, and couscous and bring to a boil. Reduce heat and simmer until the squash is cooked, 10 to 12 minutes. (The zucchini will be softer than usual.)

3   Add the fish and cook until just cooked through, about 3 minutes. Measure out 2½ cups of the hot broth mixture and add it to the bowl of couscous. Cover and let sit until all the broth is absorbed, about five minutes.

4   Remove the cilantro and ginger and serve the stew in a shallow bowl. Garnish with reserved cilantro and serve alongside couscous if desired.

✳ If you take 2 minutes in the morning to chop the onion & zucchini, you will inexplicably save 15 minutes at the other end of the day. Don't ask us how.

Sure, you can just use the regular old links, but what fun is that? Ask your butcher for Sicilian-style sausage.

active time: 5 minutes
total time: 25 minutes
serves: 4

sausage coil *with* greens & lemon

2 1-pound sausage coils
(*any kind*)

1 handful tender baby greens
(*like arugula and spinach*)

2 fat, juicy lemons

1   In separate frying pans, cook the coils for about 10 minutes per side over medium-high heat. (If you're using chicken sausage, you may want to add a tablespoon of olive oil to the pans first.)

2   Remove the sausages and plate them atop the greens. Squeeze the lemons into the pan and swirl the juice around for 10 seconds. Drizzle it over the sausages.

Securing the coil with crossed skewers (as shown) helps keep it together when it's flipped.

This classic Greek soup, thickened with eggs and spiked with lemon, is especially delicious when you add shredded chicken.

active time: 20 minutes
total time: 20 minutes
serves: 4

avgolemono

4 cups chicken broth

¼ cup uncooked orzo
(*or rice or pastina*)

salt and pepper

3 eggs

3 tablespoons lemon juice

1　In a large saucepan, bring the broth to a boil.

2　Add the orzo, rice, or pastina and cook until tender but still al dente, about 7 minutes (20, if using rice). Season with the salt and pepper and reduce heat to low; let simmer.

3　In a medium bowl, whisk together the eggs and lemon juice until smooth.

4　Ladle about 1 cup of the hot broth into the egg-and-lemon mixture, whisking to combine.

5　Add the mixture back to the simmering saucepan. Stir just until the soup becomes opaque and thickens as the eggs cook, 1 to 2 minutes. Add more salt and pepper, if desired, and serve.

 Uncooked orzo in a lidded jar = instant maraca for the toddler hanging on your apron

Everyone hits the burger-and-dogs
wall about midway through summer.
Liven up the barbecue by throwing
a few of these on the grill.

active time: 30 minutes
total time: 30 minutes
serves: 5

grilled lamb footballs

1 pound ground lamb

4 tablespoons bread crumbs, mixed with ½ cup water

2 garlic cloves, minced

1 small onion, minced

1 teaspoon salt

½ teaspoon pepper

1 egg

1 teaspoon ground cumin

1 teaspoon ground paprika (*optional*)

2 tablespoons chopped parsley

2 tablespoons chopped cilantro (*optional*)

2 tablespoons olive oil

1 cup plain Greek yogurt

1 cucumber, finely diced

⅓ cup chopped fresh mint or parsley

¼ teaspoon cumin

¼ teaspoon salt

1   Heat a grill or the broiler. Mix together all the ingredients for the lamb but the olive oil with your hands. Form the mixture into flattened ovals about the size and thickness of small hamburger patties.

2   Insert skewers as shown and brush the patties with the oil. Grill or broil them (on a lightly greased broiler pan) for about 4 to 5 minutes on each side.

3   Whisk together the dipping-sauce ingredients. Serve with the footballs.

You may have already discovered how cedar planks on the grill keep salmon moist and imbue it with rich, smoky flavor. So why limit the technique to warm-weather eating when it works just as well in a hot oven? (Make sure the vent is working.)

active time: 20 minutes
total time: 4 hours, 30 minutes (*includes soaking time*)
serves: 4

maple-glazed plank salmon *with* coconut rice

1 cedar plank (*for cooking*)

⅓ cup maple syrup

1 teaspoon Dijon mustard

½ teaspoon soy sauce

juice of 1 large lime

1½ pounds salmon fillet

2 cups chicken broth

1 13.5-ounce can light coconut milk

2 cups uncooked jasmine rice

salt

1 Soak the cedar plank in water for 4 hours; place it on a rimmed baking sheet lined with foil.

2 Preheat oven to 500° F.

3 In a bowl, combine the syrup, mustard, soy sauce, and lime juice. Put the fish in this mixture to marinate while you cook the rice.

4 In a saucepan, bring the broth and coconut milk to a boil.

5 Stir in the rice, reduce heat to low, cover, and simmer for 20 minutes.

6 Place the fish on the plank skin-side down, sprinkle it with the salt, and bake for 12 to 15 minutes, until it flakes easily but is not dry.

7 Transfer the marinade to a saucepan and heat it over low-medium heat until slightly reduced, about 3 minutes. Drizzle it over the fish before serving.

You probably have everything you need to make this in your pantry right this very minute. If you have leftover cooked vegetables in the fridge, toss them in with the onion for a few minutes.

active time: 15 minutes
total time: 15 minutes
serves: 4

whole-wheat spaghetti *with* fried onions & bread crumbs

1 pound whole-wheat spaghetti

½ cup olive oil

½ cup bread crumbs

¼ teaspoon garlic powder

1 large onion, peeled and chopped

grated Parmesan to taste

salt and pepper

1   In a large pot, boil the spaghetti.

2   Meanwhile, in a large skillet over medium-low heat, add half the oil and the bread crumbs with the garlic powder. Cook, stirring constantly, until it smells nutty and fragrant.

3   Transfer the mixture to a bowl. In the same skillet, heat the remaining oil over medium-low heat and fry the onion until browned but still crisp-tender, 8 to 10 minutes.

4   Drain the spaghetti, reserving 3 to 4 tablespoons of the water. Add the spaghetti, bread-crumb mixture, and pasta water to the onion. Toss to combine; top with the grated Parmesan, salt, and pepper; and serve.

muffin-tin meals

Just because you wear a suit and talk about collateral loan obligations all day doesn't mean you're not allowed to get excited about a cupcake tin anymore. These mini meals, all made in a muffin tin, please every diner at the table—from the 36-inch kind to the 36-year kind.

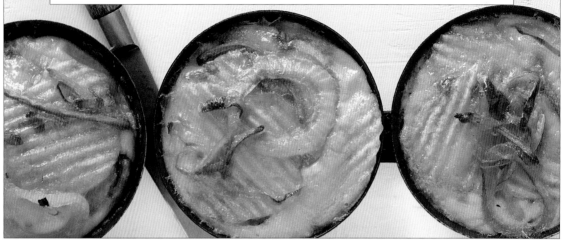

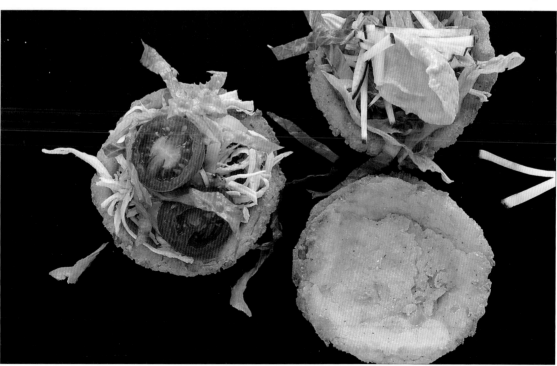

potato-chip frittata

makes: 6

5 eggs

1½ tablespoons milk
(*any fat content*)

salt and pepper

1 tablespoon olive oil

1 leek, sliced (*about ½ cup*)

½ onion, sliced (*about ½ cup*)

1 carrot, shredded (*about ½ cup*)

4 tablespoons shredded cheese
(*such as cheddar or—our
favorite—smoked provolone*)

potato chips

1 Preheat oven to 325° F. **2** Whisk together the eggs, milk, salt, and pepper; set aside. **3** Heat the oil in a skillet over medium heat. Add the leek and onion with a pinch of salt. Cook until tender, about 5 minutes. **4** Add the carrot; cook for 1 minute more. Remove from heat. **5** Grease a 6-cup muffin tin. Divide the cheese among the cups, then the vegetables. **6** Pour in the egg mixture until each cup is three-quarters full. Add a few potato chips to each. **7** Bake until cooked through, 12 to 15 minutes.

gorditas

makes: 6

1 8.25-ounce can creamed corn

½ teaspoon salt

⅔ cup cornmeal

1 tablespoon unsalted butter

½ cup shredded Jack cheese

FILLINGS OF YOUR CHOICE
**Shredded rotisserie chicken or
pork, beans, shredded lettuce,
extra cheese, chopped tomatoes,
sliced radishes, sour cream,
guacamole**

1 Preheat oven to 400° F. **2** In a saucepan over medium heat, combine the corn, salt, and ½ cup water. Whisk in the cornmeal and cook, stirring constantly, until the liquid is absorbed, about 5 minutes. **3** Add the butter and cheese, stirring to combine. Remove from heat. **4** Grease a 6-cup muffin tin. Divide the corn mixture evenly among the cups, pressing it into the bottom and up the sides to create cups. **5** Bake until crisp, 20 to 25 minutes. Let cool for 5 minutes, then turn the corn cups out of the tin. **6** Stuff them with the fillings of your choice and serve.

More muffin-tin meals on the next page →

pizza pockets

makes: 6

1 16-ounce bag store-bought pizza dough

6 tablespoons fresh or jarred marinara sauce (*such as Rao's*)

6 store-bought turkey meatballs (*such as Murray's or Trader Joe's*)

6 tablespoons shredded mozzarella

1 tablespoon grated Parmesan

1 egg

1 teaspoon milk (*any fat content*) 1

1 Preheat oven to 375° F. 2 Roll the dough out about ¼ inch thick. Cut it into sixths. 3 Grease a 6-cup muffin tin. Line each cup with a piece of dough, letting the excess hang over the sides. 4 Fill each with 1 tablespoon of sauce and 1 meatball. Divide the cheeses equally among the cups. 5 Gather each bit of overhanging dough up around the filling, pinching it together at the top. 6 Whisk the egg with the milk to make a wash. Brush it onto each pouch. 7 Bake until golden, 15 to 20 minutes.

Freeze these for up to a month for a quick microwavable dinner.

cupcake-tin pork pies

makes: 6

½ pound ground pork

½ medium onion, peeled and grated

salt and pepper

1 teaspoon chopped fresh sage

¼ cup bread crumbs

1 9-inch disc prerolled, refrigerated pie dough (*such as Pillsbury*)

1 egg, beaten

1 Preheat oven to 375° F. 2 Grease a 6-cup muffin tin with butter. 3 In a large bowl, combine all the ingredients but the dough and 1 tablespoon of the egg; refrigerate. 4 Unroll the dough and cut out 6 four-inch circles with a biscuit cutter or the rim of a drinking glass. 5 Reroll the scraps, then cut out 6 more two-inch circles. 6 Line the bottoms and sides of the tin with the four-inch rounds. 7 Divide the filling evenly among the cups. Press the two-inch rounds on top, pinching the edges together to seal. 8 Poke a hole in the center of each pie. 9 Brush with the reserved egg and bake until the tops are browned and puffed slightly, 30 to 35 minutes. 10 Let cool for 15 minutes before removing the pies. Serve warm.

These are nice with cooked apples.

Here's an adventurous idea for how to use that leftover rice from last night's takeout. If you're uneasy about the raw-fish factor with the kids, just use vegetables or cooked shrimp instead of the salmon.

active time: 30 minutes
total time: 30 minutes
serves: 4

ice-cube-tray sushi

7 ounces sashimi-grade salmon, cut into ¼-inch cubes

3 scallions, chopped

¼ cucumber, finely chopped (*3 tablespoons*)

about 5 grape tomatoes, finely chopped (*3 tablespoons*)

2 teaspoons lime juice

1 teaspoon orange juice

2½ tablespoons mayonnaise

¼ teaspoon sesame oil

¼ teaspoon salt

⅛ teaspoon pepper

2 cups cooked rice (*preferably from a Japanese or Chinese restaurant*)

1   Combine all the ingredients except the rice in a bowl.

2   To make the sushi-rice blocks, use an ice-cube tray as a mold. (Small cups, mini-muffin tins, and tartlet pans will also work.) Prepare the mold by sprinkling it lightly with water.

3   Press the rice into the tray squares, then use your finger to push a hole three-quarters of the way into each square.

4   Turn the mold upside down onto waxed paper and tap until the squares fall out.

5   Fill each hole with 2 teaspoons of the salmon mixture and serve.

If you are using rice that isn't from a Japanese restaurant, drizzle it with a mixture of the following: 3 T rice vinegar / 1½ T sugar / ½ t salt

This simple take on carbonara offers the perfect opportunity to use up leftover pasta. It also fits nicely into the category of *kids-are-asleep-spouse-is-out-and-I-get-to-eat-it-with-a-glass-of-Sancerre-all-by-myself.*

active time: 20 minutes
total time: 20 minutes
serves: 4

scrambled-egg pasta

4 eggs

½ cup grated Parmesan

8 slices thick bacon, chopped

1 onion, chopped

4 cups al dente–cooked pasta

salt and pepper

1 In a small bowl, beat together the eggs and cheese; set aside.

2 In a large skillet over medium-high heat, fry the bacon and onion together until the meat is browned and crisp and the onion has begun to caramelize, 8 to 10 minutes.

3 Add the pasta. (If using cold, day-old pasta, cook until it's just warmed through, about 1 minute.)

4 Pour the egg-and-cheese mixture into the skillet and reduce heat to low. Stir continuously until the pasta is coated with the eggs and they have begun to solidify.

5 Season with the salt and pepper, then serve immediately, with extra grated Parmesan on the side.

Also happens to make a great breakfast (it's basically bacon and eggs).

Chinese five-spice powder (made of cinnamon, star anise, cloves, fennel, and ginger) is the rich man's ketchup. It will be the flavor that gets the kids to eat anything, but it's still sophisticated enough for Mom and Dad.

active time: 15 minutes
total time: 30 minutes
serves: 4

five-spice pork tenderloin *with* cabbage *(or not)*

1 large onion (*purple or white*), **peeled and cut into thick slices**

½ head cabbage, sliced into thin wedges

1 cup apple or orange juice

1 pork tenderloin (*about 1 pound*)

2 tablespoons Dijon or spicy brown mustard

¼ cup brown sugar

1 teaspoon Chinese five-spice powder

½ teaspoon garlic powder

¼ teaspoon white pepper

1 teaspoon salt

2 teaspoons sesame oil

1 tablespoon raw or toasted sesame seeds (*optional*)

1   Preheat oven to 500° F.

2   Place the onion and cabbage in a row in the center of a small rimmed baking sheet. Pour the juice on top.

3   Slather the pork with the mustard on all sides.

4   Combine the remaining ingredients and press half of the mixture onto the pork. Sprinkle the other half over the onion and cabbage and toss.

5   Place the pork on top of the onion and cabbage and roast until the internal temperature is 150° F, about 15 minutes. Let it sit for 5 minutes before serving.

6   Pour the pan juices and the now-caramelized onions and cabbage over the pork to serve.

meatloaf 5 ways

Anyone can appreciate a recipe that demands improvisation yet is virtually impossible to mess up. In fact, meatloaf doesn't require a recipe so much as a chart that lets you choose your ingredients column by column, mix-and-match-style. On the following page, you'll see this is what we've done. Pick the meatloaf mood your family is in, and follow the simple instructions.

what meatloaf is the family in the mood for today?

	1½ POUNDS GROUND MEAT	½ CUP STARCH	½ CUP CHOPPED VEGETABLES	½ CUP SHREDDED CHEESE
❶ basic	any combo: beef, pork, veal, lamb, turkey, sausage	any combo: crackers, oats, bread crumbs, saltines, cooked grains	any combo: cooked onions, celery, leeks, shallots, scallions, bell peppers	any combo: feta, Gruyère, Parmesan, mozzarella, pecorino
❷ italian	Italian sausage and beef	seasoned bread crumbs	onions and peppers	mozzarella (only ¼ cup)
❸ asian	pork	cooked rice	scallions	—
❹ french	veal, pork, beef	bread crumbs	shallots	Gruyère
❺ thanksgiving turkey	turkey	bread crumbs	celery, onions	—

Tip: To know when your meatloaf is done, stick a knife into the middle and hold it there for 5 seconds. When you remove it, it should be too hot to hold to your wrist

1 Preheat oven to 375° F. **2** In a large bowl, using your hands, combine all the ingredients listed across one row in the chart except ¼ cup of your sauce. Pack the mixture into a greased loaf pan. **3** Bake, uncovered, for 20 minutes. Spread the reserved sauce on top and return to oven until done, another 25 minutes.

COOK TIMES

9-by-5-inch loaf pan: 1 hour, 15 minutes

Small loaf pans and muffin tins: 45 minutes, or until the internal temperature reaches 145° F

½ CUP SAUCE	EXTRAS	ALWAYS	SPECIAL INSTRUCTIONS
ketchup, mustard, hoisin, barbecue, cranberry, or pizza	–		–
pizza	½ cup milk, 1 teaspoon garlic, and 1 teaspoon dry oregano		Don't mix in the ¼ cup of cheese—sprinkle it on top during the last 5 minutes of cooking.
hoisin	1 teaspoon grated fresh ginger, and 1 teaspoon minced garlic	1 beaten egg, salt, and pepper	–
mustard (only 4 tablespoons)	3 hard-boiled eggs, ¼ cup milk, 1½ teaspoons dried thyme, and 3 slices bacon		Only put half the meat mixture into the loaf pan at first. Lay down the hard-boiled eggs end-to-end, then cover with the remaining meat mixture. Lay the bacon on top of the loaf before cooking.
ketchup (plus ¼ cup cranberry juice)	4 tablespoons dried cherries, and 8 frozen sweet-potato fries		Add 3 layers of the sweet-potato fries lengthwise in between meat layers.

An omelet is a classic example of a recipe that you should feel free to approach with abandon. This version with spring peas and leeks is delicious, but you can make it happen with just about any vegetables and herbs (asparagus, onions, tomatoes, spinach, corn) at any time of year, so long as you have eggs and cheese in the fridge.

active time: 20 minutes
total time: 20 minutes
serves: 4

spring-vegetable omelet

2 tablespoons olive oil

1 leek (*light part only*), **thinly sliced** (*about ¼ cup*)

½ cup fresh peas, blanched and drained (*or ½ cup thawed frozen peas*)

6 large eggs

1 small bunch fresh mint, stems removed, torn into small pieces

salt and pepper

2 ounces ricotta salata, crumbled (*or fresh ricotta or goat cheese*)

1   Preheat oven to 425° F.

2   Heat the oil in a large ovenproof skillet over medium heat. Add the leek and sauté until soft, then add the peas and cook for 2 to 3 minutes more.

3   Meanwhile, in a medium bowl, beat the eggs with 1 tablespoon water.

4   Add the eggs and half the mint to the pan, season with the salt and pepper, and cook, lifting the edges with a spatula to allow the uncooked eggs to flow to the bottom. When the omelet is partly cooked (5 to 7 minutes), sprinkle on the cheese and transfer the pan to the oven.

5   Bake until puffed, golden, and set, 6 to 8 minutes. Remove and allow to cool slightly. Garnish with the remaining mint to taste and serve.

bribery booty

You will not find any nutrition-ist in the world to endorse the dessert-as-leverage tactic (i.e., *If you eat your chicken, then you get a cookie!*). On the other hand, we have not found a single parent who has not relied on the strategy at some point. Redeem yourself by providing treats you feel good about.

Meyer-lemon cream pies

makes: 5

FOR THE CRUST

1¼ cups graham-cracker crumbs

2 tablespoons sugar

5 tablespoons unsalted butter, melted

FOR THE FILLING

2 12-ounce containers firm silken tofu (*such as Mori-Nu*)

grated zest and juice of 2 Meyer lemons

½ cup confectioners' sugar

1 Preheat oven to 350° F. 2 In a medium bowl, mix together all the crust ingredients. Press the mixture into the bottom and sides of 4 tartlet molds or four-ounce ramekins. 3 Bake until golden brown, 8 to 10 minutes. Remove and let cool completely. 4 In a blender, combine all the filling ingredients until smooth. Spoon the mixture into the crusts and refrigerate for at least 1 hour.

frozen chocolate bananas

makes: 4

2 ripe but firm bananas

6 ounces dark chocolate, chopped (*or semisweet chocolate chips*)

2 tablespoons vegetable oil

½ cup granola, chopped pecans and walnuts, or sprinkles (*optional*)

1 Line a baking sheet with nonstick foil or parchment paper. 2 Cut the bananas in half and insert a Popsicle stick into each half, as shown. Place them on the baking sheet and freeze for 15 minutes. 3 Meanwhile, melt the chocolate with the oil in a Pyrex measuring cup in the microwave (check it every 30 seconds) or in a half-full pan of simmering water. Stir until smooth. 4 Dip and roll each banana half in the chocolate, then quickly sprinkle with your toppings (if using). 5 Freeze until the chocolate sets, 30 minutes. Serve, or store in the freezer in an airtight container for up to a week.

apricots, yogurt & honey

serves: 2

1 ripe apricot, halved and pitted

4 tablespoons regular plain or Greek yogurt

honey

1 tablespoon unsalted roasted pistachios, roughly chopped

Top each apricot half with 2 tablespoons of the yogurt, drizzle with the honey, sprinkle with the pistachios, and serve.

fruit "cupcakes"

makes: 6 to 8

1 watermelon, cantaloupe, or honeydew melon

2 cups Greek yogurt

2 tablespoons honey

assorted food coloring

1 handful mint sprigs

assorted fruit (*strawberries, sliced bananas, blueberries, sliced kiwi, pineapple chunks*)

1 Cut the melon into large chunks. Use a scalloped biscuit cutter to create cupcake-like bases out of it. **2** Mix the yogurt, honey, and food coloring together to create frosting. Frost the melon bases with the yogurt mixture. **3** Decorate the cupcakes with the fruit, as shown.

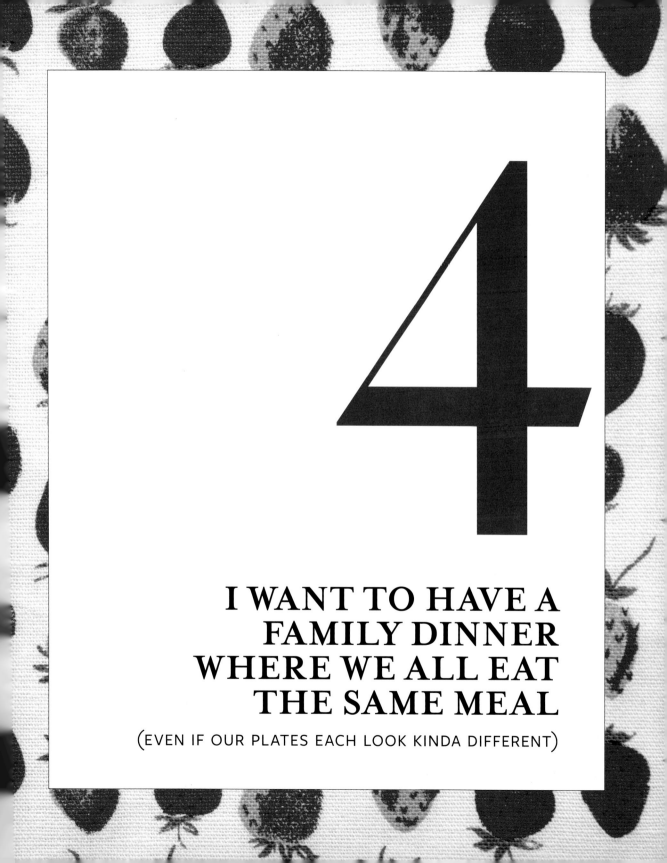

4

I WANT TO HAVE A FAMILY DINNER WHERE WE ALL EAT THE SAME MEAL

(EVEN IF OUR PLATES EACH LOOK KINDA DIFFERENT)

ARE YOU STILL TRYING TO COOK AND SERVE ONE THING THE SAME WAY FOR THE WHOLE FAMILY— ketchup-smotherer, pasta-hater, sauce-anthrope green-speck-detector be damned? No wonder you're fed up! Don't get us wrong. We're all for everyone eating the same thing, but before you go beating yourself up every night for failing to make it happen, we have some advice. Accept the fact that everyone's plate is going to look a little different, but still (how's this for magic?) cook just one meal. On the following pages, you'll see that there are all kinds of ways you can convince yourself a family meal is a universally pleasing success— even when it . . . sort of . . . isn't . . . 100 percent . . . exactly.

sesame noodles *with* extras

Start your diners with a bowl of noodles each, but let them do the customizing at the table. That way you don't have to worry about keeping track of who likes what. And even if your daughter is only interested in a pile of dry spaghetti, she's still being exposed to a dish the way it's supposed to be eaten. (She'll get it eventually.)

just sesame dressing
+ peanut butter!

nutty

1 1-pound box udon noodles or fettuccine

1 cup shredded carrots

1 hothouse cucumber, peeled and thinly sliced (*julienned, if you can handle it*)

1 bunch scallions (*whites and greens*), chopped

scallions

1 handful snow peas, sliced

1 handful peanuts, chopped

1 handful cilantro, chopped

1 rotisserie chicken, shredded

½ cup bottled Asian sesame dressing (*such as Annie's Natural*)

½ cup smooth peanut butter

shred it up

1 Prepare the pasta according to the package directions.

2 Arrange the carrots, cukes, scallions, snow peas, peanuts, cilantro, and chicken in individual bowls.

3 In a blender, mix the dressing with the peanut butter. Toss the noodles with the peanut sauce, or pour it into its own individual bowl.*

4 Serve everyone a bowl of noodles and have them customize their own meals.

* you know your family better than we do.

snappy

all the
elements

Create a bona fide grown-up salad from ingredients that are individually appealing to kids. Just be sure to plate those ingredients clustered together (and free of salad dressing) in a bowl in the middle of the table, so the kids can pick whatever combination they want.

A chicken-finger fanatic will feel right at home when he sees those gilded slices—and that's okay. The important thing is that the control shifts from you to your child, minimizing potentially epic battles while protecting the illusion of a shared meal.

classic cobb salad
with chicken fingers

FOR THE DRESSING

2 tablespoons red-wine vinegar

1 tablespoon chopped
fresh chives

1 teaspoon Dijon mustard

salt and pepper

½ cup extra-virgin olive oil

FOR THE SALAD

2 to 3 cooked chicken breasts,
sliced

4 to 5 chicken fingers
(*your child's favorite brand*)

1 bag mixed greens

3 hard-boiled eggs, sliced

5 slices bacon, cooked
and chopped

1 avocado, peeled and diced

2 handfuls cherry tomatoes

¼ cup crumbled blue cheese

1   Whisk together the vinegar, chives,
    mustard, salt, pepper, and olive oil to
    make the dressing.

2   Arrange the salad ingredients on one
    large platter so diners can pick and
    choose. Serve the dressing on the side.

all together
for you

just their favorites
(nothing touching!)

changeable
toppings

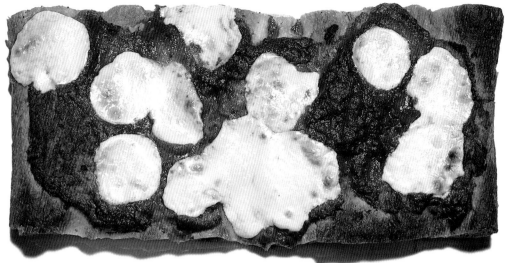

shredded
zucchini
for you

margherita
for them

Take orders from the kids before the food goes in the oven and you minimize potential tableside protests. By changing toppings every few inches, this faster-than-Domino's version becomes a meal kids and adults can get excited about. Why not just order takeout? Because you're giving them a wholesome, healthy version of their favorite and showing them that the world can be bigger than mozzarella and marinara.

please-everyone pizzas

2 tablespoons olive oil

1 sprinkle flour

1 12-to-16-ounce ball prepared pizza dough

1 small onion, chopped

1 large zucchini, shredded

salt and pepper

1 cup marinara sauce

1 ball fresh mozzarella, sliced into thin rounds

1 Preheat oven to 400° F.

2 Brush half of the olive oil onto a large baking sheet and sprinkle it with the flour.

3 Stretch the pizza dough into a 15-by-8-inch rectangle.

4 Sauté the onion and zucchini in the remaining olive oil until softened. Season with the salt and pepper.

5 Top part of the dough with the marinara sauce and fresh mozzarella, and part of it with your zucchini topping.

6 Bake the pie until the crust has browned and the cheese has melted, 25 to 30 minutes. Slice and serve.

Pizza is always a wise choice when you're entertaining families. See page 244 for more ideas!

fish "presents"

Personalized parchment-paper packets do require a little front-end focusing—Dad wants salmon, you want tilapia, the kids want anything as long as there's no lemon—but overall, it has no bearing on total prep-and-cook time. Once they get to "unwrap" their gifts at the table, all the wheeling-and-dealing and who-wants-what business is finished, and the family can just concentrate on dinner.

customized for each eater

wrap it up!

1 large (*about 12-by-15-inch*) **piece parchment paper for each diner**

1 3-to-5-ounce piece fish for each diner

chopped vegetables (*leeks, peas, cauliflower, broccoli, carrots*)

2 tablespoons olive oil

1 lemon, sliced horizontally

salt and pepper

1 tablespoon unsalted butter

1 Preheat oven to 400° F.

2 In the center of each piece of parchment paper, place a piece of fish. Top it with vegetables of your child's choosing, drizzle with the olive oil, and add a slice or two of lemon, salt, pepper, and some dots of butter. Then fold the paper to enclose.

3 Bake each package on a baking sheet for about 12 to 14 minutes. (Salmon or thicker-cut fish may take a few minutes longer.)

4 Serve each "present" on a plate and unwrap them for the kids at the table. (Be careful—the steam can be scalding hot.)

a little bit
of this

Mediterranean sampler

It looks like a well-considered Middle Eastern–themed menu, but the reality is that these bits and bites were just pulled from an end-of-the-week refrigerator. Depending on your mood and your fridge, you could just as easily head in the charcuterie direction (salami, Parmesan, olives, gherkins, crusty bread) or, even better, the wing-it direction (whatever you got).

a little bit
of that

USE LEFTOVERS SUCH AS
cheese sticks, hummus, olives, last night's meat, the doggie bag from Tuesday's dinner out, the vegetables that came home in the lunchbox untouched, deli meats, edamame, pickles, tuna.

Lunchbox Leftovers

1 Eyeball your fridge and pantry, grabbing whatever looks good.

2 Use as many different serving plates as possible to generate excitement.

3 Set "dishes" out smorgasbord-style and let everyone take what they like.

mix it up

just a
tad sweet

ready to go

a little
bit of green

You start with a leg up on this one, because slightly exotic and slightly sweet crepes conjure up happy dessert thoughts for the kids (and *joyeux* Parisian memories for you). And there's no need to overthink the fillings. This selection is especially delicious, but you can have fun experimenting with whatever you have in the fridge.

creamy

caramelized

2 medium onions, sliced

salt and pepper

4 tablespoons olive oil

1 box white mushrooms,
stems removed, sliced

1 box frozen spinach (creamed
or leaves), thawed

1 pound sliced ham

½ cup shredded Parmesan

1 8-ounce container sour cream

1 16-count package crepes
(such as Melissa's)

what
you want

what they
want

crepes

1   Set 2 medium frying pans over medium-low heat.
    In one, sauté the onions with salt and pepper in
    2 tablespoons of the olive oil until sweet and golden,
    15 to 20 minutes.

2   In the other pan, sauté the mushrooms with salt and
    pepper in the remaining olive oil, 8 to 10 minutes.
    Remove; set aside. In the same pan, cook the spinach
    until heated through.

3   In either pan, heat each crepe for about 30 seconds
    a side over medium heat, as you would a tortilla.
    Remove and keep warm on a plate tented with foil
    until it's time to serve.

4   Serve the onions, mushrooms, and spinach in
    separate bowls with the ham, Parmesan, sour cream,
    and crepes.

5   Have each diner assemble his own crepe at the table.

soba noodles

tiny bits
of meat

bubble
bubble

Yes, this meal requires a fondue pot. If you don't have one, it's worth the investment. The sheer theatrics of family dunking will get the kids (and everyone else) charged for the meal. After everything's been cooked and eaten, encourage a good slurp of the broth, which will be rich with the flavors of what you've cooked in it. Yum.

1 pound soba noodles

1 32-ounce box beef broth (*you can use chicken, but beef is better*)

2 thin slices unpeeled fresh ginger

2 garlic cloves, peeled and smashed

½ yellow onion, peeled and left in one piece

thinly sliced pork and beef tenderloin, small-diced chicken, and shrimp (*all uncooked*)

bean sprouts

kabocha squash, thinly sliced

bok choy

shredded cabbage

firm tofu

kid-friendly chopsticks

hot pot!

1 Cook the noodles according to the package directions. Let them cool to room temperature, then place them in serving bowls.

2 Combine the broth, ginger, garlic, and onion in a fondue pot on full heat and bring to a boil. Cook small amounts of the remaining meats and vegetables in the broth, placing them on top of the noodles.

Also good to have around: toasted sesame seeds, chili paste, and a slotted spoon to remove items from the pot.

veg out

Looks like
ice cream cones!

To get the kids excited about this, press seasoned sushi rice into little heart- and star-shaped molds after first spritzing the molds with water. Also, it helps if someone is fanning the rice as you add the vinegar. (Specifically, someone pint-size who has been looking for a good reason to break out the accessories in her dress-up box.)

no sushi on sushi
night? who cares!

FOR THE SUSHI RICE

2 cups japonica or short-grain sushi rice, rinsed

4 tablespoons rice vinegar

2 tablespoons white sugar

2 teaspoons kosher salt

ACCOMPANIMENTS

freshest salmon, tuna, or yellowtail (*3 to 4 ounces per person*), **thinly sliced**

shredded carrots

cubed cucumbers

cubed avocado

toasted sushi nori (*squares of dried seaweed*), **cut into smaller squares with scissors and used to make "cones"**

pickled sushi ginger (*available in specialty stores*)

seaweed

soy sauce

wasabi

chopped roasted peanuts

sliced oranges (*for dessert*)

sushi bar

1   Place the rice in a large saucepan with 2 cups water and bring to a boil. Immediately reduce heat to low, cover, and simmer until the water has evaporated and the rice is sticky, 15 to 20 minutes.

2   While the rice is cooking, place the vinegar, sugar, and salt in a small saucepan. Bring to a boil, stir, and cook until the sugar and salt have dissolved, about 1 minute.

3   Turn the hot rice out into a large bowl. Turn the rice over to cool it and add the seasoned vinegar a bit at a time. When all the vinegar is incorporated, you will have about 4 cups of sticky, seasoned rice.

4   Arrange the rice with a platter of fish and any of the remaining accompaniments.

SPINACH RAVIOLI
9-by-5 dish with alfredo sauce,
gorgonzola, chopped spinach, and
walnuts—not for the faint of heart

BLACK-BEAN RAVIOLI
two 5-by-5 dishes with half
marinara, half alfredo, plus cheddar,
corn, and diced red bell peppers

If everyone at the table goes for the same basic marinara, mozz, and ricotta lasagna, then by all means stick with it. But the genius of this lasagna recipe is that it uses ravioli sheets in place of regular lasagna noodles—so one of you can try a black-bean-and-cheddar lasagna while the other goes with the old standby, thereby seamlessly working a flavor upgrade into family dinner. The amounts given will fill a 9-by-5-inch baking dish, two 4-by-6 pans (or 5-by-5), or six 2-by-3s. But the perforated ravioli sheets will make it easy to fit noodles into whatever baking pan you've got.

BABY CHEESE
RAVIOLETTI
2-by-3s
with marinara
& mozzarella

personal-pan lasagnas

1 16-ounce container fresh pasta sauce (*see captions for examples*)

1 15-ounce box frozen ravioli (*any kind*)

2 cups shredded cheese

½ cup desired add-ins (*see captions for suggestions*)

1   Preheat oven to 375° F.

2   Assemble your lasagnas in layers in the following order: sauce, ravioli, cheese, and add-ins, making sure you always start with the sauce and end with the cheese.

3   Cover them with foil and bake for 30 minutes. Remove foil; bake for 10 to 15 minutes more.

5

DO SANDWICHES COUNT?

I CAN'T DEAL WITH A PILE OF POTS AND PANS TONIGHT

For a good part of your life, you've probably followed the protein-starch-vegetable meal mandate (except maybe during that first-apartment, only-have-beer-and-ketchup-in-the-fridge phase). And congratulations on that! But in the interest of surviving parenthood (specifically, the feeding and eating parts of it), here's what to do next: Throw the protein-starch-vegetable dinner archetype out the window. Egg sandwich? Open-face smashed avocado on sprout bread? IF THERE'S FOOD ON THE TABLE AND EVERYONE IS EATING IT, CALL IT DINNER.

For them.

For you.

These sandwiches are excellent additions to the picnic basket. Just keep the avocado spread separate until you hit the grass.

active time: 15 minutes
total time: 15 minutes
makes: 2 big sandwiches and 2 little sandwiches

avocado BLTs

8 slices thick-cut bacon

1 ripe avocado

4 tablespoons mayonnaise

juice of ½ lemon

2 to 3 tomatoes, thickly sliced

salt and pepper

4 leaves fresh basil, roughly torn

2 tablespoons olive oil

6 slices soft oatmeal or oat-nut bread, toasted

1 head Boston or butter lettuce, leaves separated

1 Fry your bacon.

2 While it's frying, cut the avocado in half and scoop out the flesh. In small bowl, mash it with the mayonnaise and lemon juice.

3 Sprinkle the tomato slices with the salt, pepper, and basil and drizzle them with the olive oil.

4 Spread each slice of bread with the avocado mayonnaise and make 3 sandwiches with the bacon, lettuce, and tomatoes. Slice 1 sandwich in half and split it between two kids' plates.

For the kids, use regular mayo instead of the avocado mayo and remove the offending crusts.

For them.

For you.

Be warned: As soon as you serve your kids a waffle-iron grilled cheese, they may never go back. But you may not want to anyway—you can use a waffle iron as a panini maker for any sandwich that calls for melted cheese.

active time: 10 minutes
total time: 10 minutes
makes: 2 sandwiches

turkey & cheddar on challah

**2 ounces cheddar,
sliced or shredded**

**2 ounces thinly sliced
smoked turkey**

4 slices challah (*or any good
thick white bread*)

1 tablespoon unsalted butter
(*at room temperature*)

**2 tablespoons peach
chutney, cranberry sauce,
or fruit preserves**

1 Preheat your waffle iron. (Or place a grill pan or heavy sauté pan over medium heat.)

2 Make 2 sandwiches with the challah, dividing the cheese and turkey evenly between them.

3 Spread the outside of each sandwich with the butter and cook both on the waffle iron. (Or fry the sandwiches in a grill or sauté pan, turning once, until the outsides are browned and the cheese has melted.)

4 Serve with the chutney, cranberry sauce, or preserves.

FOR A MAKESHIFT SANDWICH PRESS

28-oz
can →

cast iron →
skillet

sandwich →

For you & them.

We find that kids are more likely to eat a lot of little sandwiches than one big one. Whatever they don't finish for dinner, wrap up for the next day's lunchbox or snack.

active time: 5 minutes
total time: 15 minutes
makes: 2 sandwiches

egg-salad sandwiches

2 hard-boiled eggs, peeled

3 tablespoons mayonnaise

salt and pepper

4 slices soft challah or whole-wheat bread

4 tablespoons watercress, stems removed

1 Mash the eggs with a fork until crumbly.

2 Stir in the mayonnaise, salt, and pepper.

3 Assemble 2 sandwiches, dividing the egg salad and watercress evenly between them.

4 Trim the crusts and cut each sandwich into quarters.

FOR PERFECTLY COOKED HARD-BOILED EGGS

Add the eggs to a pot of lightly salted water. Bring to a boil. As soon as the water boils, remove the pot from the heat and cover. The eggs will be done in exactly 12 minutes.

For you & them.

On the day after Thanksgiving, don't mess around with turkey potpies and soups. With once-a-year leftovers as good as these, always, *always* go for the sure thing.

active time: 5 minutes
total time: 5 minutes
makes: 1 ridiculously gorgeous sandwich

the leftover sandwich

bread (*preferably white*)

any Thanksgiving leftovers
(*sliced turkey, stuffing, scalloped potatoes, sweet potatoes, green beans, cranberry sauce, gravy. . .*)

extra condiments, such as mayo or ketchup

1 Cut the bread into thick slices.

2 Assemble as shown, or actually any way you like based on what you've got. Customize it for kids by omitting the more adventurous sides and swapping the ketchup for cranberry sauce.

For you & them.

In those rare moments when you have extra lobster lying around, make sure this is how you use it. It's the sandwich with the highest rate of seafood-skeptic conversion.

active time: 15 minutes
total time: 15 minutes
makes: 4 rolls

lobster rolls

2 tablespoons unsalted butter

4 hot-dog buns

1 pound cooked lobster meat

1 stalk celery, chopped

½ cup mayonnaise
(*or to taste*)

grated zest and juice of 1 lemon

1 garlic clove, minced

½ teaspoon paprika
(*smoked or sweet*)

1 Spread the butter evenly on the cut sides of the buns.

2 Open the buns and toast them on a griddle or in a skillet. Mix together the remaining ingredients and assemble your sandwiches. Eat warm.

Shrimp works, too!

For you & them.

You haven't been able to get to Europe with the kids yet (don't worry—it'll happen!), but you can at least add this sandwich to the rotation and feel like you're, you know, just passing through the Gare du Nord.

active time: 3 minutes
total time: 3 minutes
makes: 4 sandwiches

ham & pickles on ficelle

3 to 4 tablespoons butter

1 ficelle baguette,
divided into 4 pieces
and split

1 pound ham, thinly sliced

16 cornichons,
sliced into rounds

1 Spread the butter evenly on the bread.

2 Divide the ham and cornichons evenly between the wedges. Serve with grape tomatoes, if desired.

For them.

For you.

Ham and eggs are for breakfast, but prosciutto and eggs (and anchovies, lemon, spinach . . . pile it on!) are decidedly for dinner!

active time: 30 minutes
total time: 30 minutes
makes: 2 sandwiches

prosciutto & fried-egg sandwiches

2 slices Tuscan, ciabatta, or other crusty bread

4 to 6 thin slices Parmesan

2 thin slices prosciutto

2 tablespoons unsalted butter

2 eggs

4 salted anchovy fillets, finely chopped

1 garlic clove, peeled and thinly sliced

1 handful fresh baby spinach

1 squeeze fresh lemon juice

salt and pepper

1 Preheat broiler, with the tray set at the lowest position. Broil the bread slices on one side until toasted, 1 to 2 minutes.

2 Divide the cheese and prosciutto evenly on the untoasted sides.

3 Return them to the broiler and cook, open-faced, until the prosciutto is crispy and the cheese has begun to melt, about 1 minute. Turn off broiler, leaving the sandwiches inside to stay warm.

4 In a frying pan, melt 1 tablespoon of the butter, then fry the eggs to the desired doneness.

5 Remove the sandwiches and top each with an egg.

6 Add the remaining butter to the pan and sauté the anchovies and garlic over medium-high heat, stirring constantly, until the garlic begins to soften. Add the spinach and cook until it wilts, then add the lemon juice, salt, and pepper.

7 Spoon the anchovy mixture over the sandwiches and serve.

For the kids, top with another slice of toast before serving—and think twice about omitting the anchovies. (Your child MIGHT just surprise you)

For you.

For them.

Slow-roasted fresh tomatoes elevate this chicken sandwich to something special, but you can also use sun-dried tomatoes if you didn't think to do it in advance.

active time: 40 minutes
total time: 6 hours, 40 minutes *(includes 6 hours of optional slow-roasting time)*
makes: 4 sandwiches

crispy chicken sandwiches

2 pounds vine-ripened tomatoes, sliced in half vertically and seeds removed

salt and pepper

5 tablespoons olive oil

½ cup unseasoned bread crumbs

grated zest of ½ lemon

2 teaspoons finely chopped fresh rosemary

2 tablespoons grated Parmesan

4 chicken cutlets, pounded thin *(about 8 ounces total)*

1 handful fresh baby arugula

2 small baguettes, cut in half lengthwise

1 Preheat oven to 200° F. Place the tomatoes, cut-side up, on a baking sheet lined with nonstick foil. Season with the salt and pepper, drizzle with 3 tablespoons of the oil, and bake for 6 hours. Remove and let cool. (The tomatoes can keep in the fridge for about four to five days.)

2 Preheat oven to 425° F.

3 In a shallow pan, combine the bread crumbs, lemon zest, rosemary, Parmesan, the remaining oil, and more salt and pepper. Press the cutlets firmly into the bread-crumb mixture.

4 Transfer them to a pan lined with nonstick foil and bake until browned and firm, 15 to 20 minutes. Remove and let cool, then assemble with the arugula and baguette as shown.

Use crushed pretzels instead of breadcrumbs for the kids' sandwiches.

open-face night

There are any number of circumstances that call for Open-Face Night: You're back from vacation and the refrigerator is empty. Your daughter is due backstage at six and must eat *something*, butterflies be damned. Or it's Tuesday night and you just can't deal. So slice the bread, set the table, pour the milk. Totally legit.

smashed egg & salt on toast

Smash your hard-boiled eggs (one per eater) with a fork, adding a little mayonnaise, if that's your thing. Spread the mixture on seven-grain toast and add salt to taste.

goat cheese & strawberry preserves

Use the freshest goat cheese you can find. (It spreads best at room temperature, but if it's been in the fridge for a few days, don't let that stop you.) If you aren't a fan of the sweet-tangy play, you can go with ricotta, too.

avocado on sprout bread

Mash a ripe avocado with a squeeze of lime and salt. Spread the mixture on toasted sprout bread. Top with split grape tomatoes, if desired.

sardines & lemon on white toast

Spread butter on toasted white bread (Pepperidge Farm is magical here) and top with chopped sardines, a little lemon zest, minced parsley, and minced garlic. Try to get the kids to at least take a taste.

minted-pea puree *with* mozzarella

In a mini food processor or blender, whirl ½ cup of thawed frozen peas, ¼ cup of olive oil, a handful of mint, a tablespoon of grated Parmesan, and a squeeze of lemon. Add salt and pepper to taste. Spread the mixture on ciabatta and top with mozzarella.

almond butter & baby bananas

This is tricky, so pay attention: Spread almond butter on bread and top it with sliced bananas.

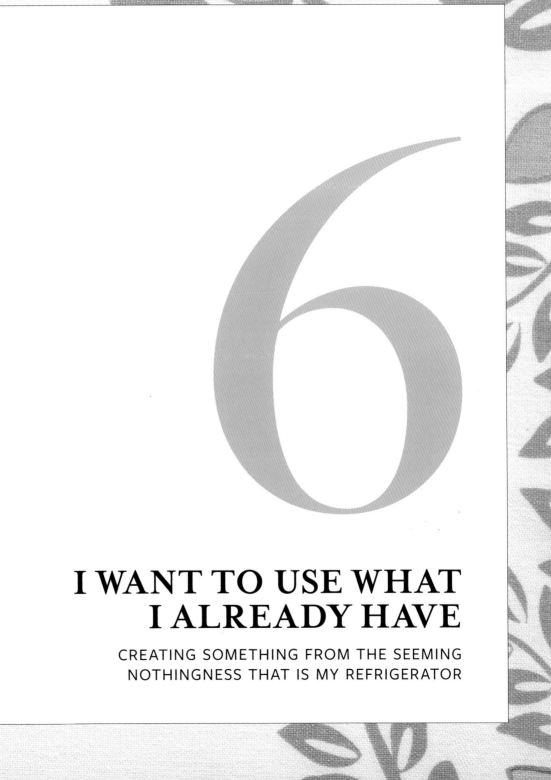

I WANT TO USE WHAT I ALREADY HAVE

CREATING SOMETHING FROM THE SEEMING
NOTHINGNESS THAT IS MY REFRIGERATOR

You spent a small fortune the other day when you went to the grocery store. So why—*how*—is it that by Tuesday, you stare into the fridge and see…nothing? You have the odd bag of lentils that you moved from your pre-kid apartment, or some exotic, beer-goggled squash that you fell so hard for when you picked it up at the farmers' market. But now that it's sitting here before you in your own kitchen, almost visibly shriveling before your eyes, you have no idea what to do with the thing. Not to worry: This chapter will show you how, with just a few pantry basics and a little pluck, dinner can be a choose-your-own adventure. START WITH ONE INGREDIENT, PAIR IT WITH WHAT YOU'VE GOT, AND IT WILL LEAD YOU TO A DELICIOUS, INSPIRED MEAL FOR FOUR.

pasta

1

In a very deep pan, warm 2 tablespoons of **olive oil** over medium heat. Sauté 1 finely chopped **onion** with a pinch of **red-pepper flakes.**

SO YOU HAVE AN
EGGPLANT

sweat your eggplant

The top and bottom dishes here require the **eggplant** to be "sweated," a process that draws out its bitterness. Simply **salt** your eggplant pieces (cubes for pasta; ¾-inch-thick rounds for "burgers"), let them sit for 30 minutes in a colander, then rinse.

garlic

FIRST

1

Preheat oven to 400° F. Prick a whole **eggplant** all over with a fork. Place it on a foil-lined pan and roast until very soft, about 45 minutes.

bread

1

Cut a **red onion** into thick slices. Bake them at 350° F on an oiled sheet for about 15 minutes, turning once; set aside.

It called to you from the farmstand, all shiny and beautiful, you swear. Now the least you can do is save it from another soggy, leaden eggplant Parm— or worse, the garbage disposal.

NOW YOU HAVE

eggplant & ricotta pasta

THEN

2
Add the cubed, sweated eggplant; a pinch of **oregano; pepper;** and a little more oil. Cook until the eggplant begins to soften. Reduce heat slightly; cover, keeping the lid ajar; and cook for 15 minutes.

3
Stir in a large can of **plum tomatoes (with juices)** and 1 tablespoon each of **honey** and **lemon juice.**

4
Bring to a boil, then lower heat and simmer, with the lid ajar, for about 35 minutes.

5
Cook the **pasta** al dente and divide it into 4 bowls. Top each bowl of pasta with the sauce and a scoop of **ricotta.**

NOW YOU HAVE

baba ghanoush

THEN

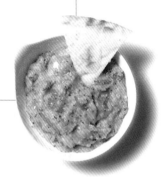

2
Let it cool for 20 minutes, then slice it in half and scoop out the flesh. Whirl 1 **garlic clove** in a food processor. Add the eggplant flesh and process until just smooth.

3
Add 3 tablespoons of **olive oil** and the zest and juice of ½ a **lemon.** Process.

4
Stir in some **parsley** (or mint). Season with **salt** and **pepper.**

5
Serve with warm **pita bread, olives, feta cheese,** and any sliced vegetables you have on hand.

NOW YOU HAVE

eggplant "burgers"

TA-DA!

2
Dredge your sweated eggplant rounds in **all-purpose flour,** a beaten **egg,** and then **bread crumbs.**

3
Heat some **canola oil** in a pan. Fry the eggplant for 2 minutes per side. Remove and drain on paper towels.

4
Top the "burgers" with **mozzarella, tomato,** and the baked onion slices. Broil until the cheese melts.

5
Place each burger on a slice of **bread** and add a dollop of **pesto** (optional).

balsamic (or red-wine) vinegar

GET STARTED

1

Stir a couple of tablespoons of **balsamic vinegar** into your cooked lentils and chill for 1 hour (if you have 1 hour).

SO YOU HAVE SOME

LENTILS

cook your lentils

Skip this step if you are making the soup. Combine 2 cups of water with 1 cup of dry **lentils** (which will yield about 2½ cups cooked). Boil for 5 minutes, then reduce heat and simmer until tender but still firm, 15 to 20 minutes.

NOTE: *Don't add salt to the water, or the lentils will taste chalky and tough.*

IF YOU HAVE

a sweet potato

1

Sauté 1 peeled, cubed **sweet potato** with some chopped **onion** and a stalk of **celery** in **olive oil** in a large stockpot for about 5 minutes.

IF YOU HAVE

salmon

1

Fry a piece of **bacon** in a medium saucepan. Remove and crumble; set aside. In the remaining fat, cook chopped **carrots, onions,** and **garlic** until soft.

The little legumes are as easy to store as a box of pasta, rich in protein and fiber, and quick to cook (no soaking required).

Mediterranean lentil salad

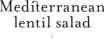

2
Combine 1 tablespoon of **balsamic vinegar**, 1 minced small **garlic clove**, 2 tablespoons of **olive oil**, and **salt** and **pepper** to taste.

3
Toss the lentils with the vinaigrette and some **chickpeas,** halved **tomatoes,** and sliced **red onion.**

4
Toss with fresh greens (**arugula** or **baby spinach**). Top with crumbled **feta** and **mint** (optional).

lentil & sweet-potato soup

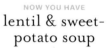
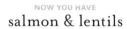

NEXT

2
Add a teaspoon each of **cumin** and **coriander** and a chopped **red bell pepper** (optional).

3
Stir in 1 cup of dry lentils and 4 cups of **chicken broth.**

4
Bring to a boil, then reduce heat and simmer for 40 minutes.

5
Stir in 2 big handfuls of **spinach** leaves. Continue cooking until the spinach is wilted. Add **salt** and **pepper** to taste.

salmon & lentils

2
Gently stir in your cooked lentils, a few **fresh thyme** leaves, and the cooked bacon. Add just enough **chicken broth** to moisten.

3
Meanwhile, sprinkle 4 **salmon** fillets (skin-side up) with **salt** and **pepper.** Heat 2 tablespoons of **unsalted butter** in a nonstick skillet over medium heat. Sauté the fish, turning once, until just cooked through, 6 to 8 minutes.

4
Mound the lentils on plates. Top with the salmon and chopped **parsley,** if you have it.

FRESH TOMATOES

At their summer peak, they need little more than a drizzle of olive oil or a sprinkling of salt to feel like a meal. The most flavorful ones will have a rich tomato aroma. And don't refrigerate them once you get home—the flesh will become mealy.

IF YOU HAVE

pasta

1

Cut 4 large, ripe heirloom or beefsteak tomatoes into bite-size pieces; place them in a bowl with the juice and zest of 1 **lemon.**

IF YOU HAVE

bread

FIRST

1

Toast 2 slices per eater of your favorite **bread.**

IF YOU HAVE

bulgur wheat

1

Cook 1 cup of the **bulgur wheat** according to the package directions; set aside. Dice 2 ripe tomatoes, ½ a small **red onion,** and 1 large peeled **cucumber.**

pasta *with* fresh tomatoes

2
Cook a pound of **pasta** according to the package directions. Drain it, reserving a cup of cooking liquid, then return it immediately to the pot.

3
Toss it with 4 tablespoons of **olive oil,** 2 finely minced **garlic cloves,** the tomato mixture, and **salt** and **pepper** to taste.

4
Stir in 4 ounces of **ricotta** or **goat cheese,** adding just enough of the pasta water to help it coat evenly.

5
Serve, topped with chopped **basil,** toasted **pine nuts,** and grated **Parmesan.**

tomato sandwiches

2
Generously spread each piece with **mayonnaise,** and layer each with thick rounds of ripe tomato.

3
Sprinkle with **sea salt** and serve, open-faced.

tabbouleh salad

2
Stir the vegetables into the wheat with ¼ cup of **olive oil,** the juice of a large **lemon,** and **salt** and **pepper** to taste.

3
Stir in ½ cup each of chopped **fresh mint** and **parsley.**

4
Serve the salad as a meal, topped with crumbled **feta.** (It will keep for up to 2 days in the fridge.)

BUTTERNUT SQUASH

Is there a tastier, more ubiquitous signifier of autumn? The bright orange flesh is full of vitamins A and C and fiber and is virtually impossible to overcook.

pasta

START

1

Cook the **pasta** (we like rigatoni) al dente.

prep the squash

Peel the tough skin, discard the seeds, and cut the flesh into small cubes. Toss with **olive oil**, a handful of sliced **onion**, fresh **thyme** (if you have any), **salt**, and **pepper.** Roast on a cookie sheet at 425° F until the **squash** is very tender and the onion is translucent and fragrant, about 40 minutes.

IF YOU HAVE
pizza dough

HERE WE GO...

1

If it's not already at 425° F, preheat your oven. Roll out a 14-ounce ball of **pizza dough** on a well-floured surface and transfer it to a warm baking sheet.

IF YOU HAVE
chicken broth

1

In small batches, blend your roasted squash with **red-pepper flakes** and a couple of cans of **chicken broth.**

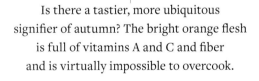

NOW YOU HAVE
pasta *with* squash & ricotta

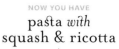

2
Meanwhile, heat the roasted squash in a large pot with more **olive oil.** Add the cooked pasta.

3
Add **salt, pepper,** and chopped **basil.** Drizzle with more **olive oil.**

4
Top with dollops of **ricotta** or **goat cheese.**

NOW YOU HAVE
pizza *with* squash & herbs

2
Sprinkle grated **mozzarella** or **Parmesan** over the dough. Scatter your roasted squash on top.

3
Season with **salt** and **pepper.**

4
Add a little **rosemary** or minced **red onion.**

FINISH

5
Bake until the cheese has melted and the crust is crisp, 25 minutes.

NOW YOU HAVE
butternut squash soup

2
Simmer, adding more stock or some **apple cider** if the soup is too thick.

3
Divide among 4 bowls. Add **salt** and **pepper,** and top with **Parmesan.** Drizzle with **olive oil.**

4
Serve with a dollop of **sour cream, chives,** or chopped **walnuts,** if desired.

baking potatoes

SWISS CHARD

1

Preheat oven to 350° F. **Butter** a 9-by-13-inch baking dish. Peel and thinly slice 2 **potatoes** (with a mandoline, if you have one).

prep the chard

Wash 1 bunch of **swiss chard** in cool water and drain. Trim the leaves from the stems, then roughly chop the leaves and pat them dry. (Don't worry about the exact size of the bunch. These recipes will work no matter what size your grocery store or farmers' market sells.)

IF YOU HAVE

linguine

GET STARTED

1

Cook the **linguine** al dente; set aside.

IF YOU HAVE

pork tenderloin

It's time to retire a few ideas you may have about dinner. Meat doesn't always require two sides, lasagna doesn't need noodles, and eggs aren't only for breakfast. In fact, a bunch of these leafy greens can yield three complete dinners that are anything but expected.

1

Place some **olive oil** in a large sauté pan over medium heat. Cube a 1-pound **pork tenderloin** and generously season it with **salt** and **pepper.**

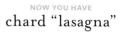

2

Layer a quarter of the slices in the dish. Sprinkle with **salt, pepper,** and a little chopped unsalted butter. Top with ⅓ of the prepped chard.

3

Layer with grated **Gruyère** or **Swiss cheese,** a pinch of **dried** or **fresh thyme** leaves, and more salt, pepper, and butter. Repeat twice.

4

Pour ½ cup of **milk** (any kind) over the top. (The pan will seem very full— don't worry, it will cook down.) Cover with foil and bake until tender, a little over an hour.

5

Remove the foil and top with a last layer of Gruyère or Swiss and, if desired, **Parmesan.** Broil until the cheese is melted and golden.

2

In a large skillet, sauté 2 minced **garlic cloves** in **olive oil** with some **red-pepper flakes** for 1 minute.

3

Add the chard and sauté until wilted; remove from heat. Add the pasta. Toss with **salt, pepper,** and a handful of grated **Parmesan.**

4

Divide the pasta among bowls and poach (or fry) 1 **egg** per serving.

5

Top each bowl with an egg and some **hot sauce,** if desired.

NOW

FINISH UP

2

Brown the pork on all sides, tossing until it's cooked through, about 8 minutes. Remove from pan; set aside.

3

Add a chopped **onion** to the pan. Reduce heat and sauté until tender.

4

Add a couple of tablespoons of **white wine** (or **white-wine vinegar**) and ½ tea-spoon of **horserad-ish.** Cook for about 1 minute, stirring.

5

Add the chard and sauté until wilted but still green. Return the pork to the pan and toss until warmed through. Serve with **crusty bread.**

cod

MISO PASTE

1

Rinse and dry 1 ½ pounds of **cod fillets;** set aside. For the marinade, boil ½ cup of **mirin** (rice wine) in a saucepan for 30 seconds. Stir in 1 tablespoon **soy sauce** (optional).

choose your miso

There are many different types of **miso paste,** but the most common are white (mellow and slightly sweet) and red (saltier and stronger). We prefer white for the recipes here.

IF YOU HAVE
tofu

1

In a bowl, combine 2 tablespoons of miso paste, 2 tablespoons of **rice-wine vinegar,** 2 tablespoons of **mirin** (rice wine), and 1 tablespoon of **sugar.**

IF YOU HAVE
a rotisserie chicken

Sweet enough to win over the kids and shelf-stable enough to last in the refrigerator for a year, that tub of antioxidant-packed soybean paste isn't just an Asian-grocery staple—it's the answer to your prayers.

FIRST

1

Shred the **chicken;** set aside.

THEN   NOW

2
Remove the marinade from heat and whisk in ½ cup of miso paste and 1 tablespoon of **honey.** Let it cool to room temperature.

3
Marinate the cod in the miso mixture in the fridge for 1 hour. (For richer flavor, let it sit overnight.)

4
Preheat oven to 400° F. Wipe excess marinade from the cod. Roast the fish until just opaque, 15 to 20 minutes.

5
As the fish cooks, reduce the remaining marinade over medium heat, 4 minutes. Serve the fish over steamed **greens** with a drizzle of sauce.

NOW

2
Stir in a little chopped fresh **ginger** and the juice of 1 **lime.**

3
Whisk in 3 tablespoons of **olive oil.** Puree the mixture with 1 **carrot** and 2 **scallions.** Cover and chill for at least 20 minutes.

4
Cube 1 package of firm **tofu.** Soak it in some of the miso dressing; set aside.

5
Toss the remaining dressing with **romaine** and whatever vegetables you have on hand (**peppers, cukes, tomatoes**). Spoon the tofu over the salad.

2
In a large stockpot, combine 2 cups of water with 5 cups of **chicken stock.** Bring to a boil, then reduce heat to medium-high.

3
Stir in a grated **carrot** and 2 ½ cups of sliced **shiitake mushrooms.** Simmer for 5 minutes, then add the chicken and heat through.

4
Stir ⅓ cup of miso paste into the broth and simmer for 3 minutes more. Serve, garnished with sliced **scallions.**

CORN

IF YOU HAVE

cornmeal

1

Preheat oven to 350° F. Separate 3 **eggs** into 2 bowls. Whisk the yolks with ⅓ cup of **milk** (any kind).

2

Into the yolk mixture, whisk a pinch of **salt** and 2 tablespoons each of **cornmeal, flour,** and **sour cream.** Stir in raw kernels from 3 ears of corn and a dash of **cayenne pepper.**

IF YOU HAVE

bacon

START

1

Fry 6 strips of **bacon** until crisp, reserving about 2 tablespoons of the drippings. Crumble; set aside.

2

Cook a 16-ounce package of **fettuccine** al dente. Drain, reserving ¾ cup of the pasta water.

IF YOU HAVE

shrimp

These three simple meals showcase sweet, crisp kernels of summer corn with minimal effort. Frozen corn can stand in as an alternate year-round.

1

Squeeze the juice of 1 **lime** and 1 **lemon** into a small bowl. Toss 1 pound of raw peeled **shrimp** with half the juice.

spoon bread

NEXT

3
Beat the egg whites on high until soft peaks form. Gently fold them into the yolk mixture.

4
Mix 1 minced, seeded **jalapeño pepper** with ½ cup of grated **Jack** or **cheddar.** Sprinkle it all inside a buttered 1-quart baking dish. Spoon the egg mixture into the dish. Top with another ¼ cup of grated cheese.

5
Bake for 25 to 30 minutes. Let stand for 3 minutes. Serve with broiled tomatoes and call it dinner.

NOW YOU HAVE

fettuccine *with* bacon & corn

COMBINE

3
Return the pasta to the pot. Add the bacon, drippings, raw kernels from 3 ears of corn, and 1 cup of grated **Parmesan.**

4
Toss to combine, adding a bit of the pasta water if it seems too dry.

5
Divide into bowls. Top each portion with chopped **basil, black pepper,** and more Parmesan.

NOW YOU HAVE

corn & shrimp salad

NEXT

2
Sauté the shrimp in **olive oil** over high heat for about 1½ minutes a side.

3
Remove the shrimp. Toss raw kernels from 3 ears of corn in the pan juices until warm.

4
Chop 2 **tomatoes,** some **cilantro,** and 1 **avocado.** Add to pan with the corn, olive oil, **salt,** and remaining juice.

5
Add the shrimp and toss once more. Serve, tossed with **Boston lettuce.**

white fish

1

Preheat oven to 425° F. Slice 2 **baking potatoes** into long wedges. On a baking sheet, toss the slices with **salt** and **olive oil.** Bake until browned, about 25 minutes.

SO YOU HAVE SOME

PEAS

prepare the peas

If you're using the frozen variety, soak a 10-ounce package in lukewarm water for about 15 minutes, then drain. If you prefer fresh, boil 1 cup of water for every 2 cups of shelled **peas,** then simmer them for at least 5 minutes to cook through. Definitely use frozen for the soup.

IF YOU HAVE

soba noodles

GET STARTED

1

In salted water, cook the **noodles** al dente. Rinse and set aside. Place the pasta pot back on the stove.

IF YOU HAVE

buttermilk

1

Wash and chop 3 tablespoons of **fresh mint** leaves.

When it comes to convenience in cooking, peas may be the gold standard. Seriously nutritious whether fresh or frozen, they keep in the freezer for months and cook up in minutes.

NOW YOU HAVE

fish & chips
with pea mash

NOW   **NEXT**

2

Meanwhile, in a saucepan over medium heat, melt 1 tablespoon of **unsalted butter.** Add the peas with some salt and **pepper.** Cook through, then remove from heat.

3

Mash the mixture with a potato masher or a fork until most of the peas are broken up.

4

Transfer the potatoes to a plate. Place 4 **white-fish fillets** (such as sole or tilapia) on the warm baking sheet.

5

Sprinkle each with **bread crumbs,** ½ tablespoon of chopped butter, and a squeeze of **lemon juice.** Broil until golden. Serve the fish alongside the mash and potatoes.

NOW YOU HAVE

pea & mushroom
soba noodles

FINISH UP

2

Thinly slice 1 small **onion** and 2 **garlic cloves.** In the pasta pot over low heat, cook the onion and garlic in **olive oil** until golden.

3

Add ⅓ cup of **mirin** (rice wine), a few tablespoons of **tamari,** and 6 ounces of sliced **shiitake mushrooms.** Cook for 5 minutes.

4

Add a 12-ounce package of **spinach** and ¼ cup of water. Toss until just wilted. Stir in the peas, a few sliced **scallions,** and the juice of 1 **lemon.**

5

Add the noodles and toss to combine. Serve immediately. (It's also delicious chilled.)

NOW YOU HAVE

chilled
buttermilk-pea soup

2

Blend together 1 cup of buttermilk, the mint, ½ cup of **chicken broth,** 2 cups of thawed frozen peas, and 1 teaspoon of **olive oil.**

3

Serve in bowls at room temperature with **salt** and a squeeze of **lemon.** (Or chill for later.)

POTATOES

Don't underestimate those Idahos and Yukons knocking around in your pantry. The fail-safe staples are packed with potassium and vitamin C—especially great news for parents whose toddlers are already on the all-white-foods diet.

IF YOU HAVE
ground turkey

BEGIN

1
In a saucepan, cover large chunks of 2 peeled Idahos with water. Bring to a boil, then simmer for 20 minutes. Drain; place them back in the pan.

2
Mash the potatoes with 2 tablespoons of **unsalted butter,** ⅓ cup of **half-and-half,** and **salt** to taste. Set aside.

take stock of your stash

Idaho (a.k.a. russet) potatoes are best for baking and mashing, while Yukon golds and reds are best when you want potatoes that hold their shape (for soups or salads, say). For each recipe, first preheat your oven to 425° F.

IF YOU HAVE
grape tomatoes

OKAY...

1
Bake 4 scrubbed and fork-pricked Idahos for 1 hour.

IF YOU HAVE
pizza dough

1
Toss 2 peeled, diced Yukon gold potatoes with **red-pepper flakes, fresh rosemary,** a sliced **garlic clove, salt,** and **olive oil.** Roast in the oven for 10 minutes.

shepherd's pie

3

Cook ½ an **onion,** 2 **carrots,** and 4 stalks of **celery** (all chopped) and 1 tablespoon of **fresh thyme** leaves in **olive oil** over low heat until tender. Increase heat slightly and add 20 ounces of **ground turkey.** Cook until meat is browned, 5 minutes.

4

Stir in ⅓ cup of **white wine** and ¾ cup of **chicken broth.** Bring to a boil. Whisk in 2 tablespoons of **all-purpose flour.**

FINISH UP

5

Reduce heat and simmer until the juices thicken, 5 to 10 minutes. Spoon the mixture into a casserole dish. Spread the potatoes over the top. Bake until golden, 15 to 20 minutes.

NOW YOU HAVE

baked potatoes *with* vegetables

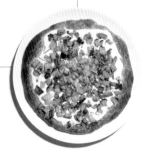

NEXT   NOW

2

Toss a carton of washed **grape tomatoes** with **olive oil, fresh oregano, salt,** and **pepper.**

3

Distribute the tomatoes on a rimmed baking sheet. Put it in the oven alongside the potatoes for the last 10 minutes of the potatoes' cooking time.

4

Continue roasting until the tomatoes burst.

5

Top the potatoes with the tomatoes, crumbled **feta,** and **kalamata olives,** or with blanched broccoli or sautéed peppers (optional).

NOW YOU HAVE

roasted-potato pizza

KIDS!
COME HELP!   NOW

2

Roll out the **pizza dough** on a baking sheet. Increase heat to 475° F and put the dough in the oven next to the potatoes.

3

Roast the potatoes and bake the dough for 10 minutes. (The potatoes will get 20 minutes total.)

4

Remove both from the oven. Spread the crust with **ricotta;** top with the potatoes and some grated **Parmesan.**

LAST

5

Return the pizza to the oven and bake until the crust is browned, about 7 minutes.

a piecrust

ARTICHOKES

OKAY...

1
Preheat oven to 375° F. Prick the bottom of the **crust** with a fork and prebake it for 8 minutes.

choose your chokes

Fresh or frozen? If you're going fresh, look for the less mature "baby" variety, which can be eaten whole with minimal prep (just steamed and halved or quartered). For the quiche here, use 8 ounces of (drained) canned or (thawed) frozen hearts. For the chicken, use 15 ounces. Use fresh for the marinated ones.

IF YOU HAVE

fresh tarragon

START

1
With a sharp knife, trim the stem and the top ½ inch of each of 4 fresh artichokes. Boil them in water for 25 to 35 minutes; drain and set aside.

IF YOU HAVE

a chicken

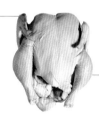

No, they're not *Shrek* action figures; they're sweet, earthy, edible thistles. But they can be just as fun for kids if you know what to do with them. As with tomatoes, some recipes work nearly as well with the canned or frozen kind—and who are we to turn down a shortcut?

1
Rinse the pieces of a quartered **chicken.** Pat dry; season with **salt** and **pepper.**

COOL

2
Panfry 2 ounces of thinly sliced **prosciutto** until crispy. Crumble it over the bottom of the crust. Evenly distribute the artichokes and 2 ounces of shredded **Gruyère** in the crust.

3
In a bowl, combine ¾ cup of **milk** (any kind) and ¾ cup of **half-and-half.** Whisk in 3 **eggs** and a few grinds of fresh **pepper.**

4
Pour the mixture into the crust. Sprinkle with 1 teaspoon of **fresh thyme** leaves.

5
Bake until a knife inserted in the center comes out clean, 35 to 40 minutes. Let rest for 10 minutes before serving.

NEXT SERVE

2
Place ½ cup of chopped **tarragon** and 1 minced **garlic clove** in a bowl.

3
Whisk in the zest and juice of 1 **lemon,** 1 tablespoon of **Dijon mustard,** and some **pepper.** Slowly add ¾ cup of **olive oil,** whisking constantly.

4
Drizzle half the marinade over the artichokes. Chill for 1 hour.

5
Serve halved, with the remaining marinade on the side for dipping.

NOW FINALLY

2
In a straight-sided skillet over medium-low heat, cook 1 sliced **onion** in **olive oil** for about 5 minutes.

3
Increase heat slightly and add the chicken to the pan. Brown it, about 3 minutes a side.

4
Add the artichokes, 1 cup of **white wine,** and a drained 15-ounce can of **plum tomatoes.**

5
Bring to a boil, then reduce heat and simmer, covered, for 1 hour. Serve in shallow bowls over **brown** or **white rice.**

CANNED TOMATOES

IF YOU HAVE
canned tuna

1
Cook 1 pound of **pasta** according to the package directions; drain and return it to the pot to keep warm.

2
In a large pan over medium heat, sauté a small chopped **onion** and a minced **garlic clove** in 2 tablespoons of **olive oil** for 4 minutes.

IF YOU HAVE
chicken

1
Salt chicken pieces (any cuts, about 1½ pounds total) and brown on all sides in 2 tablespoons of **olive oil** in a large pan over medium-high heat, about 10 minutes. Set aside.

2
In the same pan, sauté a chopped **onion,** a handful of sliced **mushrooms,** and a chopped **bell pepper** (red or green) in 2 tablespoons of olive oil for about 8 minutes.

IF YOU HAVE
shrimp

These recipes each use a 28-ounce can of peeled, whole plum tomatoes. (We're partial to the San Marzano variety.) Squish them with your hands as you drop them, with their juices, into the pan.

1
Preheat oven to 400° F. In a large bowl, toss a pound of large peeled **shrimp** with **salt, pepper,** and the juice and zest of 1 **lemon.**

fettuccine *with* tuna & capers

THEN

3

Add the tomatoes and a can of **tuna in oil**. Increase heat to medium-high and cook for 12 more minutes, stirring occasionally.

4

Stir in **salt** and **pepper** to taste and a handful of sliced **fresh basil**. Remove from heat.

5

Divide the pasta between 4 bowls and top each with sauce, a tablespoon of **capers**, and a scoop of **ricotta**. Serve.

chicken cacciatore

NEXT

3

Stir in ½ teaspoon of **cinnamon** and ½ cup of **red wine**. Cook for 1 minute, then add the tomatoes and cook for 3 minutes more.

4

Add the chicken back to the pan. Bring the sauce to a boil; reduce heat. Cover and simmer for 45 minutes, turning the pieces once halfway through.

5

Remove the chicken; set aside. Increase heat to medium. Let the sauce reduce for 15 minutes, then remove it from heat. Add chopped **basil**, **salt**, and **pepper**.

6

Serve the chicken over **noodles** (or rice) topped with the sauce.

shrimp scampi *with* feta

2

In an ovenproof skillet over medium heat, sauté 2 sliced **garlic cloves** and a minced **shallot** in 2 tablespoons of **olive oil** for 3 minutes.

3

Stir in a few tablespoons of **dry sherry**; cook for 3 minutes. Add the tomatoes and bring to a boil, then reduce heat and simmer for 10 minutes.

4

Stir in ¼ cup of chopped **fresh oregano** and some **pepper** and remove from heat. Add the shrimp to the pan, sprinkle it with ¼ cup of crumbled **feta**, bake for 15 minutes, and serve.

WHITE FISH

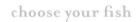

choose your fish

When buying fish for a family, a good rule of thumb is about ½ pound per adult and ¼ pound per child. These recipes work with cod, tilapia, hake, haddock, halibut, or sea bass. For the first two, use fillets with their skins removed.

There's no question that a breaded, panfried fish can be a blessing. (Show of hands for all who are still pretending it's a chicken finger?) But healthy, mild white fish deserves an expanded role in your repertoire.

IF YOU HAVE

diced tomatoes

1

In a large soup pot, sauté a chopped **onion** in 3 tablespoons of **unsalted butter** over medium heat.

IF YOU HAVE

cîtrus fruît

1

Peel and slice horizontally 3 **oranges** and 2 **lemons.** Heat ½ cup of **olive oil** in a deep sauté pan over low heat until just warm.

IF YOU HAVE

potatoes

1

Preheat oven to 400° F. Toss 3 to 4 thinly sliced **potatoes** and a little **olive oil** into a 9-by-12-inch baking dish.

fish stew

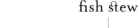

FINISH UP

2

Add a minced **garlic clove** and some chopped **fresh thyme.** Sauté until the onion is golden, about 5 minutes. Add ½ cup of **dry white wine.** Cook for 2 minutes.

3

Stir in 8 ounces of **chicken broth** (or clam juice) and a 28-ounce can of **diced tomatoes.** Bring to a boil, then reduce heat and simmer for 10 minutes.

4

Cut the fish into 2-inch chunks. Add them to the broth; cook for 3 minutes. Season with **salt** and **pepper** to taste.

5

Cook until the fish is cooked through, about 5 minutes. You can also add up to a pound of shellfish (such as shrimp, scallops, mussels, or clams), in which case cook until the shrimp are opaque and any shells have opened.

poached fish *with* citrus fruit

AND THEN...

ALMOST THERE

2

Stir in the fruit and cook until warmed through, about 3 minutes. Remove it with a slotted spoon; set aside.

3

Increase heat to medium. Place the fish fillets in the pan and season them with **salt** and **pepper.**

4

Cook them, turning gently, until just cooked through and slightly flaky, about 5 minutes on each side.

5

Divide the warm fruit among 4 plates. Top each with some fish. Sprinkle each plate with a sliced **scallion** and serve.

baked fish *with* fennel, potatoes & tomatoes

FINALLY

2

Thinly slice 1 bulb of **fennel** crosswise. Toss it with the potatoes. Season with **salt** and **pepper** and roast for 30 to 35 minutes.

3

Layer the fish (skin-side down) and 1 cup of halved **cherry** or **grape tomatoes** on top.

4

Pour ¼ cup of **white wine,** a generous squeeze of **lemon juice,** and a drizzle of olive oil over everything.

5

Season with more salt and pepper. Return to the oven and roast, loosely covered, for 15 to 20 minutes.

SAUSAGE

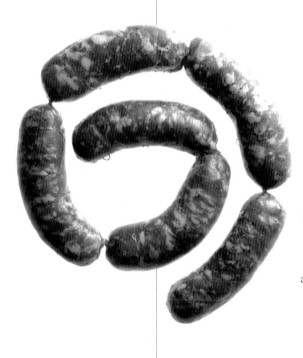

These recipes work with whichever links won you over at the butcher (though sweet or hot Italian work best for the meatballs). If you're having trouble choosing one of these dinners, freeze the sausage for up to 2 months and decide later.

prep the sausage crumbles

Skip this step if you are making the meatballs. Remove the casings from ½ to 1 pound of **sausages** and sauté, breaking the meat up with a spoon until the crumbles are brown. Set aside.

IF YOU HAVE
bell peppers

1
Preheat oven to 350° F. Cut off and remove the tops of the **peppers,** and seed, rinse, and dry them. Poke holes in the bottoms with a fork.

IF YOU HAVE
arborio rice

1
Add ¾ cup of the **rice** to some **olive oil** in a saucepan over medium-low heat. Stir to coat. Add ½ cup of **white wine** and stir until absorbed.

IF YOU HAVE
ricotta

START

1
Preheat oven to 475° F. Grease a cookie sheet with cooking spray.

NEXT

SET YOUR
TIMER

2

In a bowl, combine a beaten **egg,** some chopped **parsley, bread crumbs, marinara sauce,** and the sausage.

3

Spoon the mixture into the peppers and place them in a baking dish, then top with more sauce and toasted **pine nuts** and **Parmesan** (optional).

4

Bake until the tops are golden brown, 35 minutes.

2

Warm 4 cups of **chicken broth** in a separate saucepan or the microwave.

3

Add the broth to the rice a ladleful at a time (stirring after each addition) until absorbed and cook until the risotto tastes creamy but still firm, about 20 minutes. Add sautéed sliced **mushrooms.**

4

Add the sausage, a handful of thawed **frozen peas,** grated **Parmesan, salt,** and **pepper.** Cook until heated through.

MAKE

2

Remove the casings from 1 pound of sausages and combine the meat with ½ cup of **bread crumbs,** 1 beaten **egg,** and 3 large spoonfuls of **ricotta.**

3

Using your hands, form the mixture into 1½-inch balls.

4

Place the meatballs on the cookie sheet and bake for 15 to 20 minutes. While the meatballs are cooking, heat some **marinara sauce.**

5

Serve the meatballs and sauce with or on top of pieces of **crusty bread** with grated **Parmesan.**

SPINACH

chicken breasts

1

Cut 4 boneless, skinless **chicken breasts** into 1-inch pieces. Season them with **salt** and **pepper.** Place 2 tablespoons of **olive oil** in a large pan over medium heat.

eggs

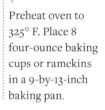

BEGIN

1

Preheat oven to 325° F. Place 8 four-ounce baking cups or ramekins in a 9-by-13-inch baking pan.

2

Divide 10 ounces of thawed frozen (or a pound of blanched fresh) spinach, a grated large **carrot**, and ½ cup of **Parmesan** among the cups or ramekins.

orzo

OKAY...

1

Prepare 8 ounces of **orzo** according to the package directions.

NOW

2

During the last minute of the orzo's cooking time, add a pound of chopped **baby spinach.** Drain; set aside.

Fresh and frozen spinach are mostly interchangeable—unless a dish, like the salad here, relies on baby spinach's just-picked texture. Keep in mind that a pound of fresh equals 10 ounces of thawed frozen.

NOW YOU HAVE
chicken saag

NOW

2

Brown the chicken pieces on all sides until cooked through, 8 to 10 minutes. Remove; set aside.

3

In the same pan, sauté a chopped **onion** in a little more oil until it's translucent. Stir in 2 tablespoons of **tomato paste.**

4

Add 2 pounds of fresh spinach by the handful (or 2 10-ounce packages thawed, frozen), stirring until it's all wilted. Add 2 table-spoons of **garam masala.** Sauté for 8 minutes.

5

Stir in 1 cup of **half-and-half.** Add the chicken back and heat until warmed through. Season with more salt and pepper and serve over **rice.**

NOW YOU HAVE
mini vegetable custards

READY?

TA-DA!

3

Add ½ tablespoon of **fresh thyme** leaves to each. Whisk 3 **eggs** with 2½ cups of **whole milk.** Add **salt** and **pepper,** then divide the mixture evenly among the cups or ramekins.

4

Add an inch of hot tap water to the baking pan. Bake until the custard tops are golden and a knife inserted at their centers comes out clean, 50 to 60 minutes.

5

Remove from oven and sprinkle each custard with a pinch of salt. Let rest for 5 minutes before serving.

NOW YOU HAVE
warm spinach & orzo salad

3

In a large bowl, combine the juice of 1 **lemon** and ¼ cup of **olive oil.** Whisk in some **salt** and **pepper.**

4

Add the orzo and spinach, along with 2 chopped **toma-toes** and a thinly sliced **red onion.** Toss to combine.

5

Stir in 4 ounces of crumbled **feta** and a handful of **pine nuts** or **walnuts;** serve.

PEACHES & PLUMS

When stone fruits are at their summer peak,
you'll want to eat them all day long.

choose your fruit

The taco and salad recipes here work with any combination of peaches, plums, apricots, and nectarines, so pick your favorites. But we do insist on the peaches for the second one.

IF YOU HAVE
white fish

1

Set oven to broil. On a baking sheet, brush 1 pound of firm **white-fish fillets** (such as tilapia) with **olive oil.** Add **salt** and **pepper** to taste; set aside.

IF YOU HAVE
pork tenderloin

1

In a bowl, combine ¼ cup of **tamari,** ½ cup of **white wine,** and ⅓ cup of **olive oil.** Whisk in 1 teaspoon of **Dijon mustard** and 2 tablespoons each of **fresh thyme** and **brown sugar.**

IF YOU HAVE
walnuts

BEGIN

1

Toast ½ cup of **walnuts** on foil in a toaster oven for 2 minutes (or in a small frying pan over medium-low heat for 4 to 5 minutes, tossing frequently).

fish tacos *with* fruit slaw

2
In a bowl, whisk 1 tablespoon of minced **ginger** with the juice and zest of a **lime,** ¼ cup of **mayonnaise,** and 2 teaspoons of **honey.**

3
Chop 1 nectarine, 2 plums, 2 **scallions,** ½ a **red onion,** and 1 seeded **jalapeño** (optional). Add everything to the dressing with more salt and pepper. Chill, covered.

4
Broil the fish until it's opaque, about 6 minutes. Meanwhile, warm 8 tortillas in a 350° F oven or a toaster oven.

5
Place the fish in the tortillas. Serve, topped with the fruit slaw and **fresh cilantro.**

grilled pork *with* peaches

THIS... IS... EASY!

2
Reserve ¼ cup of the marinade. Place 2 **pork tenderloins** in the rest, and cover and chill for 1 to 3 hours.

3
Heat the grill (charcoal or stove-top). Grill the pork, brushing it with the reserved marinade and turning once, until a meat thermometer in the thickest part of it reads 150° F, 25 minutes.

4
During the last 8 minutes of cooking, brush 4 large peach halves with the reserved marinade. Place them on the grill, cut-side down.

5
Let the pork rest for 5 minutes before slicing. Arrange it on plates with the peaches and season everything with **salt** and **pepper;** serve.

stone-fruit salad

NOW

2
In a bowl, whisk together ¼ cup of **olive oil,** ¼ cup of **orange juice,** and 2 teaspoons of **Dijon mustard.**

3
Thinly slice 4 cups of mixed fruit (about 6 pieces).

4
Toss the fruit with the vinaigrette and a few large handfuls of **mixed greens,** adding **salt** to taste.

5
Divide the salad between 4 plates, topping each with an ounce of **blue** or **goat cheese.** Sprinkle it with the toasted walnuts and serve.

GROUND TURKEY

There are reasons ground turkey is a parent's go-to protein: It's lean, freezable, and easy to season. But just how much turkey chili can one kid eat before threatening to revolt?

new potatoes

1

Cut 1 pound of **potatoes** into quarters; set aside. In a large pot, heat 2 tablespoons of **olive oil** over medium heat.

pick your protein

Buy 1 pound of **ground turkey;** look for the more flavorful dark meat or a blend of dark and white. Other ground meats— lamb, pork, beef— are also delicious in any of these recipes.

spaghetti

1

In a large pot, heat 2 tablespoons of **olive oil.**

dinner rolls

1

Preheat oven to 450° F. Sauté a handful of finely chopped **red onion** in olive oil.

    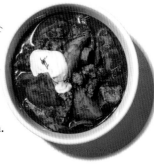

NOW YOU HAVE

turkey goulash

2
Add 4 slices of **bacon,** chopped up, to the pot. Stir until cooked. Stir in a small chopped **onion** and ¼ cup of water.

3
Add 2 tablespoons of **paprika** and 1 tablespoon of **crushed caraway seeds.** Cook until the onion is soft, about 5 minutes. Add the meat. Cook until just browned, about 5 minutes.

4
Add 2 chopped **carrots,** 1 chopped **green pepper,** the potatoes, and **salt** and **pepper.**

5
Stir in 8 ounces of **tomato sauce** and 15 ounces of **chicken broth.** Bring to a boil, then simmer, covered, for 40 to 45 minutes. Stir in 2 tablespoons of **fresh dill** and serve, garnished with **sour cream.**

NOW YOU HAVE

turkey Bolognese

2
Add 1 diced **onion,** 3 diced **celery** stalks, and 3 finely chopped **carrots.** Cook until the onion is soft, about 5 minutes.

3
Add a minced **garlic clove, salt, pepper,** and the turkey.

4
Add 2 **bay leaves,** a 28-ounce can of **tomato puree,** and 1 tablespoon of **dried oregano.** Stir in ½ cup of water; bring to a boil. Simmer for at least 30 minutes.

5
Fifteen minutes before serving, cook the pasta. Remove the sauce from heat. Take out the bay leaves, stir in ½ cup of **whole milk,** and serve with a dollop of ricotta (optional).

NOW YOU HAVE

sliders

NEXT

2
In a large bowl, combine the onion with the meat. Add **salt** and **pepper** to taste.

3
Add 1 tablespoon of chopped **fresh thyme** and 2 tablespoons of **Dijon mustard.** Combine well with a fork.

4
Form the mixture into small, flat patties. Bake them on a baking sheet until sizzling, 10 to 12 minutes.

5
Serve open-faced on split **rolls** with **lettuce** and **cranberry relish** (or, more likely, **ketchup**).

EGGS

potatoes

1

Preheat oven to 350° F. In a large ovenproof pan, sauté a pound of thinly sliced Yukon gold **potatoes** in 2 tablespoons of **olive oil** over medium heat for 10 minutes.

shrimp

1

In a bowl, toss a pound of peeled, deveined **shrimp** with 2 tablespoons each of **rice vinegar** and **soy sauce**; set aside.

2

In a large pan, scramble 3 eggs in a little **canola** or other **vegetable oil** until just cooked. Add a few more tablespoons of oil, a teaspoon of grated **ginger,** and 2 minced **garlic cloves.**

baby spinach

We believe eggs are always on the "you should" side of the question "Should I or shouldn't I buy organic?" Organic ones are way more flavorful than nonorganic and are packed with those brain-boosting EFAs.

BEGIN

1

In a large pan over medium-high heat, toss an 8-ounce bag of **baby spinach** with a little water until just wilted. Remove from heat and cover to keep warm.

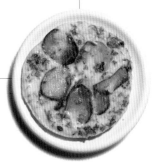

2

Add ½ a chopped **onion** and another 2 tablespoons of oil. Season with **salt** and **pepper.** Cook until the potatoes are cooked through, about 15 minutes.

3

In a bowl, whisk 6 eggs with 1 tablespoon of **fresh oregano** and ¼ cup of chopped **parsley.** Pour the egg mixture into the pan, reduce heat, and cook for 5 minutes.

4

Transfer the pan to the oven and cook for 5 to 8 minutes, until a knife inserted in the center comes out clean. Let rest for 5 minutes, then cut into wedges and serve.

3

Increase heat to high and add a finely shredded small **green** or **red cabbage.** Cook until wilted, about 3 minutes.

4

Add the shrimp to the pan; stir and cook until opaque. Stir in 2 tablespoons of **hoisin sauce** and toss for 1 minute.

5

Serve immediately, wrapped in store-bought **crepes** or over **rice.**

2

Poach or fry 4 eggs. While they are cooking, toast 4 slices of your favorite **bread.**

3

In a blender, pulse 2 egg yolks with ¼ teaspoon of **salt** until frothy.

4

Set a blender on high and slowly stream in 1 stick of melted, slightly cooled **unsalted butter** and 2 teaspoons of **lemon juice** (or sherry vinegar).

5

Top each piece of toast with the spinach, an egg, and a generous drizzle of the hollandaise. Serve with salt, **pepper,** and hot sauce, if desired.

ROTISSERIE CHICKEN

Our mothers had Hamburger Helper; we have store-bought rotisserie chickens. No matter what the season, they should be strategy number one in the family-dinner playbook.

IF YOU HAVE chicken broth

1 Finely chop 2 **garlic cloves** and ½ a large **onion.**

2 Over medium heat, sauté the onion and garlic with a 4-ounce can of **diced green chilies** (optional) in a tablespoon of **olive oil** with ½ teaspoon each of **cumin** and **chili powder** for 5 minutes.

prep your chicken

Each of these recipes calls for a 2½-to-3-pound **rotisserie chicken**, skin removed, meat pulled from the bones and shredded or cut into bite-size chunks. (It should yield about 4 cups.)

IF YOU HAVE bacon

FIRST

1 Cook 6 strips of **bacon** until crispy; crumble and set aside.

IF YOU HAVE biscuit dough

1 Bake a package of **biscuits** according to the directions. While they bake, melt 4 tablespoons of **unsalted butter** in a medium soup pot over moderately low heat.

2 Add a chopped **onion**, 3 chopped **carrots**, and 2 chopped stalks of **celery**. Sauté for 10 minutes, then whisk in 6 tablespoons of **all-purpose flour.**

3

Add 2 quarts of **chicken broth** and bring to a boil. Reduce heat and simmer for 5 minutes.

4

Add the shredded chicken and **salt** and **pepper** to taste; cook until warmed through.

5

Remove from heat and stir in a diced ripe **avocado,** a handful of chopped **cilantro,** and the juice of 1 **lime.**

6

Serve, topped with a few **corn chips** and a sprinkling of grated **cheddar.**

2

Finely chop ½ a small **red onion,** 1 large stalk of **celery,** and 2 **scallions.** In a large bowl, combine it all with the chicken.

3

Stir in a few tablespoons each of **mayonnaise** and **sour cream,** a squeeze of **lemon,** and **salt** and **pepper** to taste.

4

Serve on a bed of **Boston lettuce,** garnished with the bacon and a few **tomato** wedges.

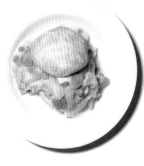

FINALLY

3

Add ½ cup of **white wine** and stir until a paste forms, about 1 minute. Slowly add 4 cups of **chicken broth,** stirring until smooth. Simmer over low heat until thickened, 5 minutes.

4

Add the shredded chicken and a handful of **frozen peas;** cook until warmed through, about 5 minutes. Season with **salt** and **pepper.**

5

Split the biscuits in half. Place the bottom halves in shallow bowls, ladle the chicken mixture over them, cover with the biscuit tops, and serve.

baby spinach

1

In a bowl, combine
½ to 1 teaspoon of
chili paste, 3 table-
spoons of **honey,**
1 tablespoon of **soy
sauce,** and a pinch
of **salt.**

TOFU

drain the tofu

All these recipes call for
a 14-ounce container
of **extra-firm tofu.** To
drain it, line a plate with
paper towels, top it with
sliced or crumbled tofu
(check each recipe for the
precise cuts), cover with
2 more paper towels,
and let sit for 10 minutes.

pork
tenderloin

1

Cut the pork into
8 medallions and
sprinkle them
with **salt, pepper,**
and **Chinese five-
spice powder.**

vegetables

1

In a large pan,
heat 3 tablespoons
of **vegetable oil**
over high heat
for 1 minute.

Since it comes in so many textures,
tofu is a godsend for kids with "consistency
issues." It's also relatively flavorless—the
rare blank canvas that's nutritionally loaded.

ALMOST THERE | FINALLY

2

In a large pan, heat ⅓ cup of **vegetable oil** over high heat for about 3 minutes. In a second bowl, place ¼ cup of **all-purpose flour.** Dredge tofu slices in the flour, shaking off any excess.

3

Fry the tofu until golden, about 2 minutes per side; set aside. Let the oil cool off for a few minutes, then pour half of it out and return the pan to medium heat. Sauté 2 minced **garlic cloves** for 1 minute.

4

Add 10 ounces of **baby spinach,** tossing it with tongs until just wilted, about 2 minutes.

5

Divide the spinach among 4 plates and top each with 2 tofu slices. Drizzle with the chili-paste mixture and serve immediately.

2

In a large pan over high heat, brown the pork in 2 tablespoons of **olive oil,** 3 to 5 minutes per side. Set aside, covered. Cook 1-inch chunks of tofu in another tablespoon of oil, 2 minutes per side; set aside with the pork.

3

Add a pound of chopped **broccoli** to the pan and stir-fry it until tender, 3 minutes. Remove and add it to the pork and tofu.

4

Deglaze the pan with 2 tablespoons of **balsamic vinegar,** stirring, for 1 minute. Stir in ¼ cup of **hoisin sauce,** then remove from heat. Pour the sauce over the pork, tofu, and broccoli; serve.

2

Add a sliced **red bell pepper** and a tablespoon of minced **fresh ginger;** sauté for 1 minute. Add 1½ cups each of **snow peas** and sliced **mushrooms** and 1 cup of thawed frozen **corn;** sauté for 2 minutes.

3

Stir in large tofu crumbles and a tablespoon each of **sesame oil** and **soy sauce.** Toss gently to combine until the tofu is heated through.

4

Stir in a few tablespoons of chopped **fresh basil** (optional). Season with **salt** and **pepper** and serve immediately.

APPLES

You've made your pies and your purees
for baby . . . now what to do with
the other bushel you brought home?

pork chops

1

Season 4 eight-ounce **chops** with **salt,
pepper,** and a dash of **cumin.** In a large
skillet over medium-high heat, brown the
chops in a tablespoon of **olive oil,**
4 to 5 minutes per side.

choose
your fruit

Crisp, tart varieties
(such as Granny Smith,
Gala, and McIntosh)
work well for these
recipes. Begin by
coring 2 large apples.

Cornish game
hens

1

Preheat oven to
425° F. Melt 2 table-
spoons of **unsalted
butter** in a large
pan, and add 4 sliced
scallions. Cook
until soft, about
2 minutes.

chicken
breasts

1

Slice 2 large **chicken breasts** into 1-inch
strips. In a large pan, brown the strips in
2 tablespoons of **olive oil** over medium-
high heat, 8 to 10 minutes; remove and
set aside.

pork chops *with* apples & thyme

THEN TA-DA!

2
Remove the chops from the pan; set aside, covered. Pour out half the pan juices. Return the pan to heat and cook a chopped **onion** for 5 minutes.

3
Reduce heat to medium. Add thick apple rounds to the pan with a few sprigs of **fresh thyme** and a tablespoon of **cider vinegar.** Cook for 5 minutes, scraping browned bits from the pan.

4
Return the chops to the pan and cover; cook for 10 to 12 minutes, turning once, until the meat is cooked through.

5
Spoon the apples and onions onto 4 dinner plates, top each with a chop, and serve.

ſtuffed Cornish game hens

NOW

2
Add ½-inch chunks of apples to the pan with a tablespoon of **dried thyme** leaves. Cook for 4 minutes, stirring. Add ⅓ cup of **chicken broth;** cook for 2 minutes.

3
Remove the pan from heat. Add 3 cups of crumbled **corn bread** and ¼ cup of chopped **pecans,** tossing gently to combine.

4
Place 4 **game hens** on a rimmed, lightly greased baking sheet. Spoon some stuffing into the cavity of each hen and tie the legs with butcher twine.

5
Sprinkle the hens with **salt** and **pepper.** Dot each with butter. Bake until the juices run clear, 1 hour. Remove the stuffing and spoon it onto plates. Place a hen on each and serve.

chicken curry *with* apples

2
Add a chopped **red onion,** reduce heat, and cook for 3 minutes, stirring occasionally.

3
Add ¾-inch apple chunks to the pan with a tablespoon of **orange juice** and 1 to 2 table-spoons of **curry powder.** Cook until the apples are tender, 4 minutes.

4
Stir in a 24-ounce can of **coconut milk** and the chicken. Simmer until slightly thickened, 6 to 8 minutes.

5
Serve, spooned over steamed **jasmine rice** and sprinkled with chopped **cashews,** if desired.

chicken broth

NOW

1

Shred your vegetables (almost any work—equal amounts of carrots, celery, and onions make a good base). Greens can simply be torn up.

2

Bring 4 cups of the **broth** to a boil. (Vegetable broth or water work, too.)

WILTING VEGETABLES

IF YOU HAVE

canned whole tomatoes

1

Mince 2 **garlic cloves,** plus equal amounts of your vegetables (chopped **onions, carrots, celery,** and even grated **squash** work best).

No matter how carefully you plan your weekly shop, by Friday the Garden of Eden in your crisper has turned into a sorry collection of orphaned mushrooms and onion halves.

Before your lettuce turns to liquid, fuel a little creativity with your waste-based guilt.

IF YOU HAVE

pancake mix

1

Finely chop any combination of vegetables (spinach, zucchini, peppers, carrots, onions, garlic) to yield 2 cups.

2

In a frying pan over medium-low heat, sauté the vegetables in **olive oil** until soft. Add **salt** and **pepper** to taste.

grated-vegetable soup

3

Toss your grated veg mixture and greens into the broth and return it to a boil (by which time the veggies will mostly be cooked through).

4

Stir in 2 tablespoons of **grits** (or Cream of Wheat), 2 tablespoons of **olive oil,** and **salt** and **pepper** to taste. Simmer until thickened, 10 to 15 minutes.

5

Serve with grated **Parmesan** or **Gruyère,** if desired.

poached eggs in tomato sauce

2

In a medium saucepan, sauté the vegetables in a generous amount of **olive oil** until the onions are translucent, about 5 minutes.

3

Add the **tomatoes** (a 28-ounce can, plus a little more, if you have it) to the pan with some **red-pepper flakes** and **salt** to taste.

4

Cook over medium heat for 15 to 20 minutes.

5

Top the sauce with poached or fried **eggs.** (You can also spoon it over fish or pasta, or thin it with broth to make a soup base.)

vegetable fritters

3

While the veggies cook, prepare the **pancake batter** in a mixing bowl according to the package instructions.

4

Remove the vegetables and mix them into the batter. Add a few spoonfuls of grated **Parmesan,** if desired. (Oil the pan well if you do.)

5

Increase heat to medium. Spoon the batter into the pan in pancake-size dollops, flipping each when it's golden and crispy.

6

Serve with **salad** or a store-bought **rotisserie chicken.**

7

LET'S ALL HAVE A PLAYDATE

WHEN YOU'RE ENTERTAINING, THINK CASUAL:
THE COUNTERTOP IS THE NEW DINING-ROOM TABLE

In our parents' day—or maybe even in our pre-kid days—there was capital-E Entertaining. The menu (including starters and desserts) was carefully considered, and there was probably a whirlwind tidying-up, as well as a dishwasher run to make sure the wineglasses were free of spots. These days, it's less about the planning and perfection and more a chance to remind you and your friends that you're all in this parenting thing together. In fact, lately, we've espoused a philosophy that might liberate you from any old-school hang-ups of the pressed-napkin variety: The countertop is the new dining-room table. Have the kids crank out some pasta or beat down some pizza dough, pour some Pinot for Mom and Dad, and get the place messy. **THE LESS PERFECT YOU TRY TO MAKE YOUR EVENING, THE MORE PERFECT IT WILL BE.**

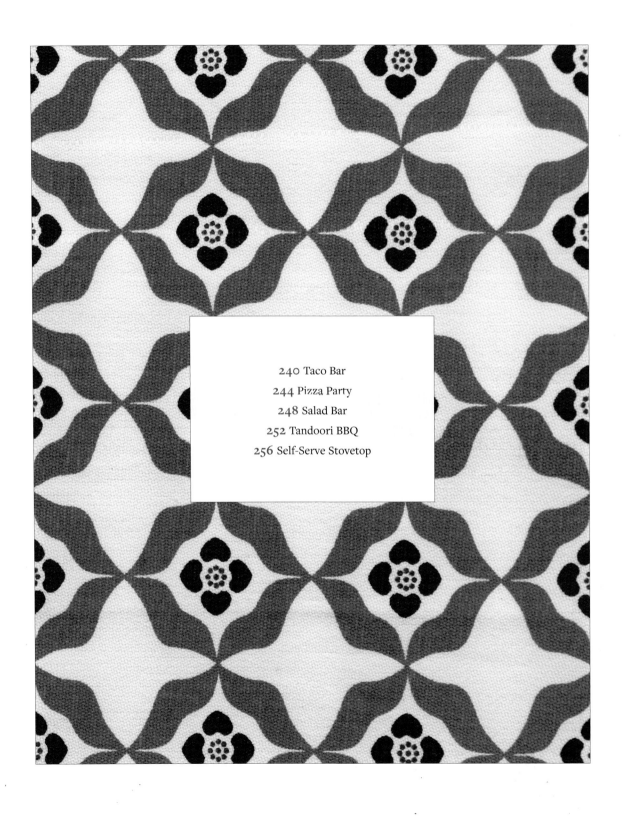

taco bar

A few strategically placed baskets of soft corn tortillas, kept warm inside your most colorful tea towel, will get everyone started on helping themselves.

THE MENU

soft corn tortillas

FILLINGS

shredded chicken *with* mole, shredded pork, black beans

TOPPINGS

tomatillo salsa, pico de gallo, guacamole, sour cream, roasted corn

EXTRAS

lime wedges, slivered radishes, cilantro

1 SHREDDED CHICKEN WITH MOLE

active time: 30 minutes | *total time:* 1 to 1½ hours | *makes:* 6 cups (enough for 10 tacos)

1 medium onion, diced

1 sprig fresh oregano
(or ½ teaspoon dried)

1½ tablespoons olive oil

4 boneless chicken breasts (*about 1½ pounds*), **cut into thirds**

½ teaspoon salt

1 cup chicken broth

1 14-ounce can diced tomatoes

¼ cup mole (*from a jar, unless you happen to have fresh*)

1 chipotle chile in adobo, seeded and minced, such as La Consteña (*optional*)

In a large, heavy-bottomed pot, cook the onion and oregano in the olive oil for 2 minutes over medium heat. Add the chicken and salt and cook until the meat is lightly browned. Add the broth, tomatoes, mole, and chile (if using). Cover and simmer for 1 hour. Remove the meat. Simmer the sauce over low heat, uncovered, for 5 minutes. Shred the chicken and return it to the sauce.

If you can't find mole, substitute a blend of ¼ cup of salsa, ½ teaspoon of cinnamon, ½ teaspoon of cumin, and a ½ teaspoon of cocoa powder.

7 SHREDDED PORK

active time: 20 minutes
total time: 1½ to 2 hours
makes: 8 cups (enough for 12 tacos)

—

1 large onion, diced

6 garlic cloves, crushed and minced

3 sprigs fresh thyme

1 sprig fresh oregano
(or ½ teaspoon dried)

1 teaspoon ground coriander

2 bay leaves

½ teaspoon salt

½ teaspoon pepper

1 tablespoon olive oil

1 3-pound boneless pork
shoulder, cut roughly into
3-inch chunks

1 14-ounce can diced tomatoes

2 chipotle chiles in adobo sauce,
minced (such as La Costeña)

juice of 1 lime

—

In a large, heavy-bottomed pot,
cook the onion, garlic, thyme, oregano, coriander, bay leaves, salt, and
pepper in the olive oil for 5 minutes
over medium heat. Add the pork,
tomatoes, chiles, lime juice, and
1¼ cups of water. Cover and simmer until the meat is tender, about
1½ hours. Transfer the meat to a
plate and shred it using 2 forks
while the sauce simmers. Add the
meat back to the sauce and simmer
for 2 to 3 minutes more. Pick out
the bay leaves before serving (in
the pot on a trivet on the countertop, or right on the stovetop if
you're not worried about the kids).

8 TOMATILLO SALSA

active time: 15 minutes
total time: 20 minutes
makes: 1¼ cups

—

2 tablespoons olive oil

4 garlic cloves, crushed

1 jalapeño, seeded and chopped

3 cups chopped tomatillos
(about 5 large)

1¼ teaspoons salt

2 tablespoons roughly chopped
red onion

½ cup cilantro

1 tablespoon lime juice

—

Heat the oil in a pan and add the
garlic. Cook until it starts to color,
then add the jalapeño, tomatillos,
and salt. Cook over medium-high
heat until the tomatillos start to
go translucent, 4 to 5 minutes.
Remove from heat and let cool for
15 minutes. In a blender or food
processor, blend the remaining
ingredients with the tomatillo
mixture until just combined.

9 GUACAMOLE

active time: 10 minutes
total time: 10 minutes
makes: 4 cups

—

4 ripe avocados, halved and pitted

juice of 1 lime

¾ teaspoon salt

1 small red onion, finely chopped or
minced (¾ cup)

1 tomato, diced (½ cup)

3 tablespoons roughly chopped
cilantro

½ teaspoon ground coriander

—

Scoop the avocados into a bowl
and mash them with a fork or
potato masher. Add in the remaining ingredients and mash until
you reach the desired consistency.
(We like it slightly chunky.)

You don't have to make all
these fillings and toppings
from scratch. Do what you can,
then buy the rest.

pizza party

If you're feeling especially ambitious—or looking for a rainy-day activity—go ahead and make the dough from scratch (it keeps in the freezer for up to 3 months). Otherwise, use store-bought dough, or pick up a large ball (about a pound and a half) from your local pizzeria and save your energy for prepping the toppings.

THE MENU

MAKE-YOUR-OWN PIZZAS

basic margherîta
prosciutto, arugula & fontina
ham & pineapple
meatball & sausage
ricotta, potatoes & truffle oil
blue cheese, onion & bacon

1 PIZZA DOUGH

active time: 10 minutes | *total time:* 1 hour | *makes:* three 8-inch round pizzas or two 14-by-10-inch rectangular pizzas

3½ teaspoons active dry yeast
(about 1½ packages)

1½ tablespoons honey

3 tablespoons olive oil

1 teaspoon salt

2¼ cups all-purpose flour

1 cup whole-wheat flour

In a large bowl, dissolve the yeast in 1 cup of warm water. Add the honey and olive oil and let sit until it becomes foamy, 2 to 3 minutes. Combine the salt with the flours and stir them into the yeast mixture a cup at a time. Turn the dough out onto a floured board and knead it for 2 minutes. Put it into a greased bowl and cover. Let it rise until it doubles in size, about 1 hour. (See the following pages for baking instructions.)

2 CARAMELIZED ONIONS
Over low heat, sauté 2 sliced onions in olive oil for 30 to 45 minutes.

3 MEAT
Precooked meatballs and Italian-sausage crumbles will go fast!

4 CHEESE
Fresh mozzarella makes all the difference.

5 GRATED ZUCCHINI
For each zucchini, grate in 1 garlic clove, a drizzle of olive oil, and a pinch of salt.

6 SLICED PINEAPPLE
The kids will love it— with or without ham, with or without pizza.

7 PIZZA SAUCE

total time: 25 minutes
makes: 3½ cups, enough for three 8-inch round pizzas or two 14-by-10-inch margherita pizzas

—

2 tablespoons olive oil

1 large onion, finely chopped (1½ cups)

3 garlic cloves, finely chopped

1 teaspoon salt

¼ teaspoon black pepper

2 tablespoons roughly chopped basil

1 tablespoon fresh oregano (or 1 teaspoon dried)

2 tablespoons tomato paste

1 28-ounce can crushed tomatoes

—

In a medium saucepan, heat the oil and add the onion and garlic. Cook over medium-low heat until the onions turn translucent, 6 to 7 minutes. Add the salt, pepper, herbs, and tomato paste; stir until well mixed. Add the crushed tomatoes. Simmer over low heat for 10 minutes, stirring occasionally. Place the saucepan on a trivet on the counter, or ladle a few cups of sauce into a large bowl and set out with the rest of the toppings.

8 TOPPINGS

Set out as many as possible to inspire creativity. Most will also serve as snacks while you wait for dinner.

—

CHEESES
shaved Parmesan

crumbled blue cheese

fresh ricotta

fresh mozzarella

Italian fontina

MEATS
cooked chorizo or sausage

cooked bacon

salami

ham

precooked meatballs

VEGGIES & FRUITS
arugula

spinach

caramelized onions

grated zucchini

sliced peppers

thinly sliced red potatoes (tossed in olive oil with thyme and sea salt)

sliced tomatoes

sliced pineapple

EXTRAS
olives

minced jalapeños

capers

red-pepper flakes

truffle oil (use sparingly; it's strong)

9 PUT IT ALL TOGETHER

total time: 20 minutes
makes: three 8-inch round pizzas or two 14-by-10-inch (the size of a typical sheet pan) rectangular pizzas
serves: 6 to 8

—

If you have the space, set up two stations: one for prepping, with all the toppings, and another for cooling and slicing the finished pizzas.

FOR EACH PIZZA, YOU NEED ABOUT:
1-pound, 10-ounce ball of dough

cornmeal (for dusting)

a few cups pizza sauce

2 cups cheese

toppings (½ cup to 2 cups each)

—

Preheat oven to 425° F. Divide the dough into halves or thirds and roll or pat them out into circles or squares on a floured surface. (It should be rolled out to about ¼ to ½ inch thick.) Place them on a greased, cornmeal-dusted cookie sheet. Top with the desired cheese, meats, and extras (see "menu" on previous page for suggestions) and bake for 20 minutes.

salad bar

This menu is ideal for summer, since everything can be made ahead and served cold or at room temperature. Think of it as a rich man's salad bar—more than just lots of options, it's lots of delicious options—and set out the bounty on one long table, preferably alfresco, with lots of small plates to encourage sampling.

THE MENU

beet & carrot slaw
pita-bread panzanella
smashed artichoke hearts
tuna-stuffed peppers
strawberries *with* basil

EXTRAS

pitas, chips, crudités,
grilled toast, potato salad

---

1 BEET & CARROT SLAW

active time: 15 minutes | *total time:* 1½ hours, including marinating | *serves:* 10 to 12

1 tablespoon sugar

juice of 2 limes

2 tablespoons white-wine vinegar

⅓ cup olive oil

¾ teaspoon salt

4 tablespoons chopped fresh mint

2 tablespoons chopped fresh parsley

4½ cups grated peeled raw beets
(*about 4*)

3 cups shredded carrots (*about 5*)

Mix the first seven ingredients together in a bowl. Add the shredded vegetables; toss to coat. It's best if the slaw chills in the fridge for an hour or two before serving.

2 POTATO SALAD

Choose American-style with mayo or Euro-style with olive oil and a splash of vinegar.

3 PITAS

Cut them into wedges and warm them in foil in a 350° F oven, or toast them to a crisp.

4 CRUDITÉS

Slice up whatever fresh veggies you've got that can be eaten raw.

5 TOAST ON THE GRILL

A day-old baguette is ideal for this. Slather it with olive oil and grill it.

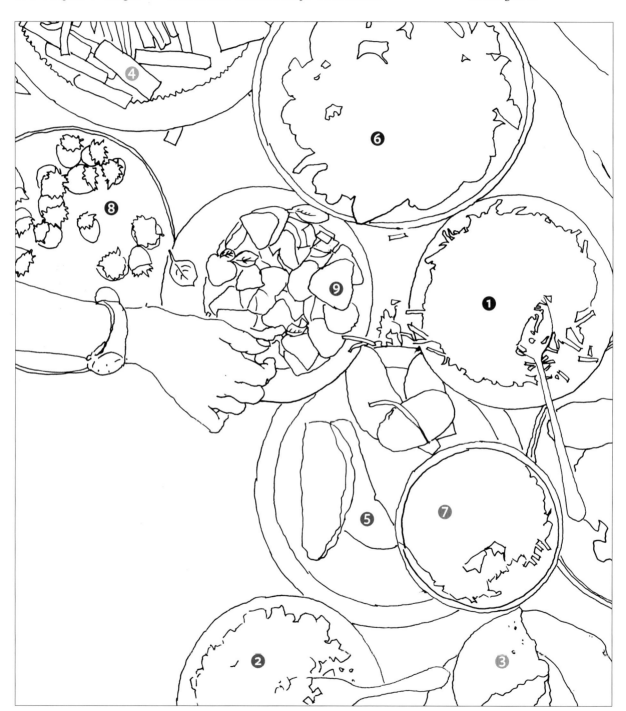

6 PITA-BREAD PANZANELLA

active time: 20 minutes
total time: 20 minutes
serves: 8 to 10

—

FOR THE DRESSING

½ cup plain yogurt

½ cup olive oil

½ teaspoon salt

1 tablespoon red-wine vinegar

1 teaspoon salt

½ teaspoon pepper

FOR THE SALAD

4 pieces pita bread (*preferably a bit stale*), torn into bite-size pieces

4 vine-ripened tomatoes, cut into wedges

1 cucumber, diced

½ red onion, sliced

1 green pepper, sliced

½ cup chopped scallions

—

In a large bowl, whisk together all the dressing ingredients. Toss in the salad ingredients.

7 SMASHED ARTICHOKE HEARTS WITH LEMON ZEST

active time: 10 minutes
total time: 10 minutes
serves: 6 to 8

—

2 14-ounce cans artichoke hearts, drained and cut into quarters

¼ cup olive oil

zest and juice of 1½ lemons

½ teaspoon salt

¼ teaspoon pepper

½ garlic clove, finely minced

2 teaspoons minced parsley

freshly grated Parmesan

—

Using a fork, smash the artichoke hearts against the side of a large bowl. Add half the olive oil and the lemon zest and juice, salt, pepper, and garlic and smash a little more. Stir in the remaining olive oil and the parsley and Parmesan.

You might consider setting aside a bowl of plain berries for green-phobic kids.

8 TUNA-STUFFED PEPPERS

active time: 15 minutes
total time: 15 minutes
serves: 6 to 8

—

2 5-ounce cans tuna in olive oil

2 tablespoons capers, drained

½ teaspoon salt

1 teaspoon Dijon mustard

2 tablespoons lemon juice

1 tablespoon roughly chopped parsley

½ small red onion, minced

1 14-ounce jar Peppadew peppers, drained

—

Mix all the ingredients but the peppers together. Using a small spoon, stuff each pepper with the tuna mixture.

9 STRAWBERRIES WITH BASIL

active time: 10 minutes
total time: 10 minutes
serves: 8 to 10

—

2 pounds strawberries, sliced

4 tablespoons basil, chopped

2 tablespoons olive oil

1 pinch salt

1½ teaspoons balsamic vinegar

—

Combine all the ingredients. Serve alone or with ice cream as dessert.

tandoori bbq

The tandoori marinade here is all you need to get through the summer grilling season—just switch up the proteins to keep it interesting.

THE MENU

tandoori-style grilled meat
or shrimp
grilled-potato smash
shrimp & mango salad
yogurt granîta

1 TANDOORI-STYLE GRILLED MEAT OR SHRIMP

active time: 20 minutes | *total time:* 4½ hours (includes marinating) | *serves:* 6

1 cup plain yogurt

1 bunch cilantro, stems removed

6 garlic cloves, peeled

1 3-inch piece fresh ginger, peeled and cut into chunks

½ medium onion, peeled and quartered

3 tablespoons garam masala

juice of 3 large limes

salt and pepper

2 pounds lamb chops, chicken breasts *(cut into 1-inch pieces and skewered)*, or shrimp *(peeled and deveined)*

In a blender, puree the first 8 ingredients. In a large bowl, toss your protein with the marinade. Chill for at least 4 hours or overnight. When ready to cook, heat the grill and shake any excess marinade from the protein.

COOK TIMES

Chops: 4 to 5 minutes a side
Chicken: 6 to 8 minutes a side on a covered grill
Shrimp: 4 minutes a side

1 TANDOORI GRILL

If you're feeling ambitious, make chicken, lamb, *and* shrimp so there will be something for everyone.

2 CASHEWS

They complement this menu perfectly. Set out several small bowls for noshing before, during, or after the meal.

3 DRINKS

Pair this meal with a fruity cocktail like mango martinis or (for the kids) classic orange soda.

4 GRILLED-POTATO SMASH

active time: 15 minutes
total time: 1 hour
serves: 6

—

2 pounds assorted tiny potatoes
(such as fingerling, new, purple, and Yukon gold)

4 tablespoons olive oil

2 teaspoons salt

8 garlic cloves, peeled

2 teaspoons ground cumin *(optional)*

2 large lemons

2 cups plain Greek yogurt *(or regular yogurt, strained overnight)*

—

Preheat grill, or preheat oven to 475° F. Combine the potatoes, oil, salt, garlic, and cumin seeds (if using) and divide the mixture between 2 large lengths of aluminum foil. Fold and scrunch up the sides of each to form 2 well-sealed pouches. Place the pouches directly on the hot grill (or on a baking sheet in the oven) until the potatoes are soft, 40 to 45 minutes. Dump the pouch contents into a large bowl and squeeze the lemons over everything. Smash the potatoes with a fork, stir in the yogurt, and serve.

5 SHRIMP & MANGO SALAD

active time: 15 minutes
total time: 15 minutes
serves: 6

—

1 pound tandoori-style grilled shrimp *(see recipe on previous page),* **chopped**

3 large mangoes, peeled and cut into chunks

½ red bell pepper, minced

½ small red onion, thinly sliced

3 tablespoons chopped cilantro

½ jalapeño, seeded and chopped *(optional)*

¼ cup olive oil

juice of 2 large limes

salt

—

Place all the ingredients but the salt in a large bowl. Stir to combine. Season with the salt and serve.

6 YOGURT GRANITA

active time: 10 minutes
total time: 3 hours
serves: 6

—

1 10-ounce package frozen strawberries, thawed with their juices, *(or 1 quart fresh strawberries)*

2 cups fruit yogurt *(we're partial to strawberry or lemon)*

—

In a large bowl, smash the strawberries into the yogurt, stirring to combine. Pour the mixture into a shallow pan (a metal baking pan works) and place it in the freezer, uncovered, for 1 hour. Remove the pan from the freezer and stir the yogurt well, breaking up any clusters of ice crystals that have formed. Return it to the freezer. Continue stirring every half hour, breaking up new clusters as they form, until the granita is completely frozen but scoopable, about 2 more hours. Scoop and serve, garnished with fresh berries, if desired.

If you have fresh mint on hand, mix a finely chopped handful of it into the yogurt and berries before you start freezing.

self-serve stovetop

Some dishes beg the question: Why even bother transferring this one to a serving platter? (It's a night with friends, not the Savannah Garden Club.) These four warm-your-bones classics can stay right on the burner, so you can outsource the serving to guests. Provide the utensils and a stack of bowls by the stovetop, add a salad and some bread if you like, and your part is done.

THE MENUS

| maple baked beans | spaghetti *with* veal-ricotta meatballs | smoked-salmon chowder | pot roast |

MAPLE BAKED BEANS

active time: 5 minutes | *total time:* 6 hours | *serves:* 6

1 pound dried navy or great northern beans

2 tablespoons brown sugar

2 teaspoons salt

¼ teaspoon pepper

2 tablespoons spicy brown mustard

2 tablespoons molasses

¼ cup ketchup

½ cup pure maple syrup

2 thick strips bacon

In a large pan, cover the beans with water by about a ½ inch. Bring them to a boil and simmer until tender, about 1 hour. Preheat oven to 300° F. In a bowl, combine everything else except the bacon. Stir in the beans. Place 1 bacon strip at the bottom of a large ovenproof dish or Dutch oven. Pour the bean mixture over it, then nestle in the other strip. Add just enough boiling water to the pot to cover everything. Cover the pot with aluminum foil, then a lid. Bake for 5 hours, checking hourly to make sure the beans aren't drying out. (Add more water as necessary to keep them just barely submerged.) Uncover for the last half hour to brown the top, if desired.

When made correctly, these meatballs are light, airy, and a little delicate to handle, so make sure the grown-ups are doing the serving. This recipe serves about four, but doubles nicely if you need more.

SPAGHETTI WITH VEAL-RICOTTA MEATBALLS

active time: 45 minutes | *total time:* 1 hour | *makes:* 12 large meatballs

FOR THE BRAISING SAUCE

3 tablespoons unsalted butter

1 large yellow onion, finely chopped

1 stalk celery, finely chopped

2 garlic cloves, minced

salt and pepper

1 bay leaf

2 cups tomato juice

2 cups chicken stock

FOR THE MEATBALLS

1 cup fresh bread crumbs

½ cup whole milk

¾ cup ricotta

¼ cup freshly grated Parmesan

¼ cup chopped fresh parsley

1 large egg, lightly beaten

salt and pepper

1½ pounds ground veal

1 16-ounce box spaghetti

Heat the butter in a Dutch oven over medium heat. Add the onion, celery, and garlic and cook for about 10 minutes. Season with the salt and pepper. Add the bay leaf, tomato juice, and stock; simmer for 20 minutes. While the sauce is simmering, combine the bread crumbs and milk in a small bowl; let them sit for 5 to 10 minutes. In a medium bowl, combine the ricotta, Parmesan, parsley, egg, salt, and pepper. Stir in the crumb mixture with a wooden spoon until well combined. Gently work the veal into the mixture. Shape the meat into large balls, packing them loosely. When the sauce is ready, reserve half a cup, reduce heat to medium-low, and carefully add the meatballs to the pot. Spoon the reserved sauce over the meatballs and cover the pot. Simmer for 20 minutes, then carefully turn the meatballs over with a large spoon. Spoon more sauce over the tops, cover, and simmer until they are firm to the touch, 15 to 20 minutes more. Make the spaghetti according to the package directions and serve alongside the meatballs.

The meatballs can be kept warm in the sauce over very low heat for about an hour.

Simple to make, this soup can also work as a healthy weeknight meal. The kids will enjoy some oyster crackers on the side, if you have them. Grown-up guests will need only a crusty baguette.

SMOKED-SALMON CHOWDER

active time: 15 minutes | *total time:* 30 minutes | *serves:* 6

—

1 tablespoon olive oil

3 medium leeks (*white and light green parts only*)**, rinsed and sliced** (*about 3 cups*)

1 garlic clove, minced

1 large russet potato, peeled and cubed

1 large stalk celery, chopped

½ teaspoon salt

½ teaspoon pepper

2 cups vegetable broth

2 tablespoons tomato paste

2 cups milk (*any fat content*)

8 ounces smoked salmon, flaked

½ cup heavy cream

2 tablespoons chopped chives

—

In a large, heavy-bottomed pot, heat the olive oil over low heat. Add the leeks and garlic and sauté for 2 minutes. Add the potato, celery, salt, and pepper and cook over medium heat for about 1 minute, stirring constantly. Add the broth and simmer until the potato is tender, about 15 minutes. Add the tomato paste and milk, then the salmon, and bring the mixture back to a simmer for a few minutes. (Don't let it boil, or the milk will separate.) As it simmers, stir in the cream. Remove from heat and garnish with the chives.

This is a huge hit when served on the stovetop during a (non-drop-off) birthday party. The guests' parents will appreciate having something to eat besides leftover pizza.

Make this New Mexico–style roast in the afternoon (the hardest part will be cracking open the can of beer). Then, when the guests arrive, you will have nothing left to cook, and the house will smell divine.

POT ROAST WITH HOMINY & SWEET POTATOES

active time: 15 minutes | *total time:* 4 hours | *serves:* 6

—

1 3-pound beef-chuck roast (*ask your butcher to tie it*)

1 tablespoon olive oil

salt and pepper

1 15-ounce jar red enchilada sauce

1 12-ounce can light beer or lager

1½ cups low-sodium beef broth

2 sweet potatoes, peeled and cut into chunks

2 small squash (*preferably chayote*), **quartered**

1 15-ounce can hominy, drained (*look for it in the canned vegetable or Hispanic section of your supermarket*)

—

Preheat oven to 450° F. Rub the meat with the oil, salt, and pepper. Place it in a baking pan and roast for 30 minutes, turning once halfway through. Reduce heat to 350° F. Add the enchilada sauce, beer, and 1 cup of the broth. Cover with foil and cook for 2½ hours, adding more broth as the liquid evaporates. Add the potatoes, squash, and hominy. Cook for 30 minutes more. Uncover and cook until the vegetables are tender and the juices are slightly thickened, 15 minutes. Carve the meat across the grain, or let the guests carve pieces themselves. (The meat will fall off the bone.) Make sure everyone gets a healthy drizzle of sauce over everything.

BOYLE & GARDNER

p. 34, p. 144: fruit cupcakes, p. 194-95: eggplant, eggplant and ricotta pasta, baba ghanoush, eggplant burgers, p. 196-97: lentils, lentil salad, soup, salmon and lentils, fresh tomatoes, p. 198-199: pasta and fresh tomato, tomato sandwich, tabbouleh salad, squash, p. 201-202: pasta, pizza, soup, Swiss chard, p. 203-04: lasagna, linguine, hash, miso paste, p. 204-05: tofu, rotisserie chicken, cod, tofu salad, miso soup, corn, p. 207-08: spoon bread, fettuccine, salad, peas, p. 209: fish and chips, noodles, chilled soup, p. 211: shepherd's pie, baked potato, pizza, artichokes, p. 213: quiche, marinated artichokes, chicken and artichokes, p. 215-16: fettuccine, chicken cacciatore, shrimp scampi, white fish, p. 217-18: fish stew, poached fish, baked fish, sausage, p. 219-220: peppers, risotto, spinach, p. 221-222: custards, orzo salad, peaches and plums, p. 223: fish tacos, grilled pork with peaches, stone-fruit salad, p. 224-25: ground turkey, new potatoes, goulash, Bolognese, sliders, p. 227: tortillas, shrimp, eggs Florentine, p. 229: tortilla soup, chicken salad, potpies, p. 231-32: tofu with spinach, tofu with pork, tofu scramble, apples, p. 233-34: pork chops, game hen, chicken curry, wilting veggies, p. 235: grated-vegetable soup, poached eggs in tomato sauce, vegetable fritters

LEVI BROWN

p. 31: blender soup, p. 84

ANDREA CHU

p. 126, p. 128: pizza pockets

CN DIGITAL STUDIO

p. 28, p. 30-31: avocado, butternut squash, sweet potato, peach, muffins, squash soup, Bellinis, p. 32-33, p. 35, p. 38-39, p. 62-63, p. 194-95: pastas, olive oil, onion, red-pepper flakes, oregano, pepper, plum tomatoes, honey, lemon, ricotta, garlic, parsley, salt and pepper, pita bread, olives, feta cheese, bread, red onion, flour, egg, bread crumbs, canola oil, mozzarella, tomato, p. 196-97: balsamic vinegar, garlic, olive oil, salt and pepper, chickpeas, tomatoes, red onion, baby arugula, mint, feta, sweet potato, onion, celery, cumin, coriander, chicken broth, spinach, salmon, bacon, carrots, thyme, butter, parsley, p. 198-99: pasta, olive oil, garlic, salt and pepper, ricotta, basil, pine nuts, Parmesan, bread, mayo, sea salt, bulgur wheat, red onion, cucumber, lemon, mint, parsley, p. 200-01: pasta, olive oil, salt and pepper, basil, ricotta, pizza dough, egg, salt and pepper, rosemary, red onion, chicken broth, red-pepper flakes, apple cider, Parmesan, sour cream, chives, walnuts, p. 202-03: baking potato, butter, salt and pepper, Swiss cheese, thyme, milk, Parmesan, linguine, garlic, olive oil, red-pepper flakes, egg, hot sauce, pork tenderloin, onion, white-wine vinegar, horseradish, p. 204-05: cod, mirin, honey, greens, rice-wine vinegar, sugar, ginger, lime, olive oil, scallions, carrots, romaine, pepper, cucumber, tomato, chicken stock, carrots, mushrooms, p. 206-07: cornmeal, egg, milk, flour, sour cream, salt, cayenne pepper, jalapeño, cheddar cheese, tomato, bacon, pasta, Parmesan, basil, pepper, shrimp, lime, lemon, olive oil, avocado, cilantro, lettuce, p. 208-209: white fish, potato, salt, olive oil, butter, pepper, bread crumbs, soba noodles, onion, garlic, mirin, tamari, mushrooms, spinach, scallions, lemon, buttermilk, mint, chicken broth, p. 210-11: ground turkey, butter, half and half, salt, carrots, celery, thyme, olive oil, white wine, chicken broth, flour, tomatoes, oregano, salt and pepper, feta, olives, pizza dough, red-pepper flakes, rosemary, garlic, ricotta, Parmesan, p. 212-213: piecrust, prosciutto, Gruyère, milk, half and half, egg, pepper, thyme, tarragon, garlic, lemon, mustard, olive oil, wine, tomato, p. 214-215: canned tomatoes, canned tuna, pasta, garlic, onion, olive oil, salt and pepper, basil, capers, ricotta, chicken, mushrooms, pepper, cinnamon, red wine, noodles, shrimp, lemon, shallot, sherry, oregano, feta, p. 216-7: tomatoes, onion, butter, garlic, thyme, white wine, chicken stock, salt and pepper, lemon, orange, olive oil, potatoes, scallion, fennel, p. 218-19: bell pepper, pepper, egg, parsley, bread crumbs, marinara sauce, arborio rice, olive oil, white wine, chicken broth, mushrooms, Parmesan, peas, salt and pepper, ricotta, bread, p. 220-21: chicken breasts, salt and pepper, olive oil, onion, tomato paste, garam marsala, half and half, rice, eggs, carrots, thyme, Parmesan, milk, orzo, lemon, tomato, red onion, feta, nuts, chicken saag, p. 222-23: white fish, olive oil, salt and pepper, ginger, lime, mayo, honey, scallion, red onion, jalapeño, tortillas, cilantro, pork tenderloin, tamari, white wine, mustard, thyme, sugar, walnuts, orange juice, mustard, greens, salt, blue cheese, p. 224-25: olive oil, bacon, onion, paprika, carraway seeds, carrots, green pepper, salt and pepper, tomato sauce, dill, sour cream, spaghetti, celery, garlic, bay leaves, oregano, tomato puree, milk, dinner rolls, red onion, thyme, mustard, lettuce, p. 226-27: eggs, potato, onion, olive oil, salt and pepper, oregano, parsley, shrimp, rice vinegar, canola oil, ginger, garlic, cabbage, hoisin sauce, crepe, spinach, bread, salt, butter, lemon, hot sauce, pepper, p. 228-29: rotisserie chicken, garlic, onion, chicken broth, cumin, chile pepper, chilis, salt and pepper, avocado, cilantro, lime, chips, cheddar, bacon, red onion, celery, scallion, mayo, sour cream, lemon, lettuce, tomato, butter, carrots, flour, white wine, peas, p. 230-31: tofu, spinach, chili paste, honey, soy sauce, salt, vegetable oil, flour, garlic, pork, salt and pepper, Chinese five spice, olive oil, broccoli, balsamic vinegar, hoisin sauce, ginger, sesame oil, p. 232-33: pork chop, salt and pepper, cumin, olive oil, onion, thyme, cider vinegar, Cornish game hen, butter, scallion, dried thyme, chicken broth, corn bread, pecans, red onion, orange juice, curry powder, coconut milk, rice, cashews, p. 234-35: chicken broth, celery, onion, carrots, grits, olive oil, salt and pepper, Parmesan, canned tomatoes, garlic, red-pepper flakes, salt, egg, pancake mix, cucumber, lettuce, red pepper, garlic.

CRAIG CUTLER
p. 40-41, p. 43-53

HANS GISSINGER
p. 178

YUNHEE KIM
p. 128: pork pies, p. 130, p. 140, p. 142, p. 144: apricots, yogurt, honey, p. 262

NGOC MINH NGO
p. 108, p. 110

MARCUS NILSSON
p. 8, p. 10-11, p. 13-15, p. 18-19, p. 22-23, p. 26, p. 54-73, p. 75-76, p. 78, p. 80, p. 82, p. 86, p. 88, p. 90, p. 92, p. 94, p. 96, p. 98, p. 100, p. 102, p. 104, p. 106, p. 112, p. 114, p. 116, p. 118, p. 120, p. 122, p. 124, p. 132, p. 134, p. 136-7, p. 146-7, p. 149, p. 160: crepes, spinach, Parmesan, mushrooms, ham, cream cheese, p. 161-69, p. 171, p. 180, p. 182, p. 186, p. 188-89, p. 192-93, p. 195, p. 219: sandwich, p. 236-37, p. 239-240, p. 244, p. 248, p. 252, p. 256, p. 258, p. 260, p. 264

MARIA ROBLEDO
p. 172, p. 174, p. 176, p. 184

TOM SCHIERLITZ
p. 31: roasted sweet potato with miso-scallion butter, p.150-154, p. 156-159

KENJI TOMA
p. 160: onions

CREDITS & ACKNOWLEDGEMENTS

WE'D LIKE TO THANK

Lia Ronnen, our project manager at Melcher Media, whose job morphed from All-Star Editor to Friend for Life almost instantly, plus the rest of the gang at Melcher Media: Charlie Melcher, Duncan Bock, and Lauren Nathan.

The brains at Chronicle, especially our editor, Lorena Jones, who got it right from the get-go.

Cookie's creative team, especially Kirby Rodriguez, *Cookie's* design director, who presided over the project like a lion watching over his young, and Linda Denahan, the most organized, least flappable person on the planet.

The design team at Number Seventeen: Bonnie Siegler, for her spot-on conviction, and the one-stop-shop Jessica Zadnik, who not only worked on every single page but also provided the sweet illustrations.

The shoot crew: Karen Evans, Kristina Holmes, Rachel Haas, and Alex Grant at Divine Studios.

The recipe crew: Melissa Vaughan, Cyd Raftus McDowell, and Frances Boswell.

Mrs. Thomson's first-grade class at Springhurst Elementary, for being nice enough to draw pictures of their favorite foods for us in the name of "visual research."

The entire Cookie staff, for putting up with nine months of extracurricular demands, particularly Julie Alvin, Joyce Bautista, Kristina DiMatteo, Sarah Engler, Cherie Gallarello, Carl Germann, Shanna Greenberg, Alex Grossman, Mireille Hyde, Myles McDonnell, and Aja Nuzzi.

Edward Klaris, Tanya Isler, and *Tamara Kobin* at Condé Nast. Without their support, there would literally be no book.

ABOUT THE AUTHORS

Pilar Guzman is the creator of momfilter.com and the founding editor of *Cookie.* She lives in Brooklyn, NY, with her husband and two boys and believes anyone can learn to put something delicious on the table.

Jenny Rosenstrach, the former food and features editor at *Cookie,* has written and edited for numerous national publications, including the *New York Times,* *Real Simple,* and *Martha Stewart Living.* She is the founder of DinnerALoveStory.com and the mother of two girls.

Alanna Stang is the executive editor of *Martha Stewart Living,* the former executive editor of *Cookie,* and the author of *The Green House: New Directions in Sustainable Architecture* (Princeton Architectural Press, 2005). She lives in Brooklyn, NY, with her husband and son, for whom she cooks (nearly) every day.

THIS BOOK WAS PRODUCED BY

MELCHER MEDIA

124 West 13th St., New York, NY 10011
melchermedia.com

PUBLISHER: Charles Melcher
ASSOCIATE PUBLISHER: Bonnie Eldon
EDITOR IN CHIEF: Duncan Bock

EXECUTIVE EDITOR / PROJECT MANAGER: Lia Ronnen
ASSOCIATE EDITOR: Lauren Nathan
PRODUCTION DIRECTOR: Kurt Andrews
PRODUCTION ASSISTANT: Daniel del Valle
EDITORIAL ASSISTANT: Coco Joly

THIS BOOK WAS DESIGNED BY

Number 17, NYC
number17.com